The Gang Life: Laugh Now, Cry Later

T0133709

The Gang Life: Laugh Now, Cry Later examines the criminal gangster mindset and offers gang prevention strategies, using real-world examples to demonstrate a holistic approach toward combatting this surging societal problem. The text outlines the evolution of gang membership from a state of interest, to association, to hardcore, "O.G." (Original Gangster) status, and explores the evolution of law enforcement's multi-pronged approach to combating criminal street gang violence, from the catch-and-release mentality of the 1970s and 1980s to today's collaboration with private organizations such as Boys & Girls Clubs.

In-depth profiles, case studies, and lengthy histories of gangs, gang members, and their transformations are provided to demonstrate the deleterious effect of gangs on society. Designed for criminal justice students and for practitioners in the field, this text offers readers a holistic approach toward gang prevention from three nationally awarded educators and gang investigators.

Robert Matthew Brzenchek is a Ph.D. student at Capella University with a proposed dissertation focus on gang research. He is an Assistant Criminal Justice Professor in Philadelphia, PA, where he educates the next generation of criminal justice professionals. He received his undergraduate degree from George Mason University and a Master's Degree from the American Military University.

As a police officer and Navy Intelligence Specialist, Brzenchek has worked with dozens of national agencies, governments, and international organizations, and has performed suppression and intervention techniques with various gangs ranging from MS-13, Bloods, Crips, and Latin Kings. He is a member of the West Point Society of Philadelphia, and Board member of SERAPH. He has published articles on gangs, emergency management, threat assessments, and homeland and international security.

Ben Pieper is a former United States Marine who was honorably discharged from the United States Marine Corps. After leaving the Marines, Pieper joined the Bradenton Police Department; he was later re-called by the USMC and returned to active duty for a tour in Iraq. Once his active duty was completed, he returned to continue his work as a law enforcement officer. Pieper is Co-Owner and Instructor for All Is One International, LLC, as well as a Detective in the Bradenton Police Department Gang Unit.

Prior to establishing All Is One International LLC, Pieper taught for the Florida Gang Investigators Association. He has worked in numerous cities nationwide, and has trained thousands of law enforcement, military, and private security personnel on topics such as criminal street gangs, racketeering, and advanced long-term investigations. In 2010, both the Florida Gang Investigators Association and the Tampa Bay Marine Air-Ground Task Force (MAGTF) honored Pieper with their Gang Investigator of the Year awards.

Garrick Plonczynski has been employed with the Manatee County Sheriff's Office since 1998. He currently is a detective and served in his agency's gang unit from 2002–2015. He is also the Co-Owner and Instructor for All Is One International, LLC. He holds a B.A. in Criminal Justice from SUNY Brockport.

Plonczynski has been the lead investigator on two R.I.C.O. cases and consulted for outside jurisdictions on their racketeering cases. Additionally, he has trained law enforcement across the nation on the threat of gangs and has been considered a subject matter expert on this topic in several high profile court cases. In 2008, he was awarded the award of Gang Investigator of the Year by the Florida Gang Investigators Association (FGIA). In 2006 and 2011, the FGIA also awarded Gang Unit of the Year to the gang unit in which he served.

The Gang Life: Laugh Now, Cry Later

Suppression and Prevention

Robert Matthew Brzenchek, Ben Pieper, and Garrick Plonczynski

Routledge
Taylor & Francis Group

NEW YORK AND LONDON

First published 2018
by Routledge
711 Third Avenue, New York, NY 10017

and by Routledge
2 Park Square, Milton Park, Abingdon, Oxon, OX14 4RN

Routledge is an imprint of the Taylor & Francis Group, an informa business

© 2018 Taylor & Francis

The right of Robert Matthew Brzenchek, Ben Pieper, and Garrick
Plonczynski to be identified as authors of this work has been asserted by
them in accordance with sections 77 and 78 of the Copyright, Designs
and Patents Act 1988.

Library of Congress Cataloging-in-Publication Data
Names: Brzenchek, Robert Matthew, author. |
Pieper, Ben, author. | Plonczynski, Garrick, author.
Title: The gang life: laugh now, cry later: suppression and prevention /
Robert Matthew Brzenchek, Ben Pieper, Garrick Plonczynski.
Description: 1 Edition. | New York: Routledge, 2018. |
Includes bibliographical references and index.
Identifiers: LCCN 2017016694 | ISBN 9781138103030 (hardback) |
ISBN 9781498778077 (pbk.) | ISBN 9781315158181 (eISBN)
Subjects: LCSH: Gangs—United States. |
Gang prevention—United States.
Classification: LCC HV6439.U5 B79 2018 | DDC 364.106/60973—dc23
LC record available at https://lccn.loc.gov/2017016694

ISBN: 978-1-138-10303-0 (hbk)
ISBN: 978-1-4987-7807-7 (pbk)
ISBN: 978-1-315-15818-1 (ebk)

Typeset in Goudy
by codeMantra

Contents

Forewords

Times of great change are always times of uncertainty—but also of great opportunity and hope. That reality has led to the extraordinary collaboration of Robert M. Brzenchek, Chief Executive Officer, All Source International Security, and Garrick Plonczynski and Ben Pieper from All Is One International, LLC. *The Gang Life: Laugh Now, Cry Later: Suppression and Prevention* provides 21st-century evidence-based insights, wisdom, and advanced strategies that address the need for greater development of "best practice" standards for managing gang life and its challenges of today and tomorrow.

Though the authors write from diverse perspectives and present their own thoughts, they weave a coherent tapestry of themes and security strategies that has helped dozens of national and global emergency management agencies, governments, the military, major corporations, educational institutions, ports, public utilities, and diverse communities on security matters, risk management, policy, and technology.

Amid the unprecedented social, demographic, and economic changes, one thing remains constant—from suppression to prevention—our obligation to advance technologies and information sharing to detect gang life from schools to careers and violations of international laws.

We believe that the time is right for global collaboration action across the public, private, law enforcement, community, and social sectors. A healthy society depends on all five sectors performing effectively with high-productivity gang intervention and prevention trauma-informed care.

Legacy Pathways' trauma-informed care, Tame and Train Your Tongue®, bullying, violence, drug, and gang prevention programs, along with leading industry organizations such as the National African American Drug Policy Coalition, the Philadelphia Anti-Violence Coalition, Strengthening the Mid-Atlantic Region for Tomorrow: PA, NJ, DE, MD/DC, law enforcement, and civic engagement organizations have greatly benefited from integrating "best practices" and lessons learned from *The Gang Life: Laugh Now, Cry Later: Suppression and Prevention.*

In tenuous times, we all know that there are no quick or easy answers. But one thing is for sure, applying the knowledge learned from this book will help shape the future for a better tomorrow. Our promise is the authors provide knowledge that can make a difference in your organizations, schools, communities, and the world.

Dr. Joi C. Spraggins, President
Legacy Pathways, LLC

****

Robert Brzenchek is an exceptional professional that I have known and worked with for many years. Over the years Bob has impressed me with his desire to learn, to increase his real-world understanding of criminal justice, and of policing issues. A great leader must have a desire to learn and grow his skills—Bob is a true leader.

Along with his student mentality he is a great teacher having created from scratch an exceptional Criminal Justice program at Peirce College. In his career he has reached top levels in the U.S. Navy, Washington DC police, and various federal agencies. Most recently he has distinguished himself as a national Gang Intervention/Intelligence expert.

This book—I predict—will become one of the key research and actionable sources for all law enforcement professionals and public policy makers. Bob has given a gift of knowledge to those on the ground fighting each day against the evil scourge of gang violence.

Dale Yeager
Forensic Profiler / CEO SERAPH

Acknowledgments

After a series of conversations we decided that we could merge the practitioner and educator worlds in a gang book. When we offered a gang symposium at Peirce College in Philadelphia, coupled with formal/informal research, we knew there was definitely interest in this approach. We then pursued the opportunity given to us to publish a book by CRC Press/Taylor & Francis. We would like to thank our families and the contributors to this book: Dale Yeager, Lauren Laielli, Benjamin Mannes, Cassondra Flanagan, Xavier Beaufort, Dr. Joi C. Spraggins, and CRC Press/Taylor & Francis.

Introduction

The first objective of gang prevention is to rectify the social imbalance in society. Gangs undeniably commit crimes and are a menace to every United States citizen; issues are increasingly changing and impactful of Criminal Justice policy and procedures. The key to social imbalance is to embrace issues of criminologists, policy makers, and criminal justice practitioners who are not receptive to holistic approaches. Holistic approaches include stakeholders identifying risk factors and implementing programs surrounding socio-economics, education, and environment with youth at the elementary school grade levels. Although overall crime rates have decreased in the last several years across the United States, gang-related crimes remain alarmingly high.

Recidivism rates in the meantime, continue to rise, with up to half of all new prison inmates incarcerated for reoffending after their initial release (Matz, Wicklund, Douglas, & May, 2012). It should come as no surprise that lower socio-economic communities contribute to gang participation, more so than higher socio-economic communities. As such, criminal justice professionals must identify vulnerabilities within those communities, in order to implement predictive gang prevention programs. As a result of the negative societal impacts of gangs, some criminal justice and public health leaders are seeking to develop new theories/methodologies in order to effectively address these challenges (Matz et al., 2012). The aim of this book is to demonstrate that a prevention strategy comprised of holistic methods is the most effective way to thwart gang violence/participation/recruitment, etc.

Prior literature in the last two decades on gangs has been an influential information tool to awareness regarding the need for gang prevention reform. Predictive gang prevention programs have no clear consensus on which model is most effective. Unfortunately, information flow about gang activity is circumspect at best. Due to the fact that there is limited evidence concerning the effectiveness of prevention programs, to be successful we must place a high priority on using collaboration and coordinating resources to effective identify prevention programs and policies and to build a body of knowledge to guide future policies and programs (Haegerich, Mercy, & Weiss, 2013, p. 417).

The age-old question on why someone would join a gang started when caveman banded together to hunt, gather, and protect. Disenfranchised African-Americans and other ethnic minority groups in American society banded together to maintain their way of life. GIs coming back from WW II formed motorcycle clubs and traversed the countryside which eventually evolved into what we now know as the Outlaw Motorcycle Gangs. In present day, various groups band together to attain Maslow's hierarchy of needs. The groups suspend rational behavior and devolve into violent mobs to acquire at all costs sex, money, power, and respect. History often dictates the future. If you do the same thing expecting different results, you are doomed to fail. So, what can you as the reader take away from this book? The following is just a brief list of content that you should walk away with:

- Obtain a road map for thwarting gang activity—every step from prevention to suppression.
- Develop an understanding of the substantive gang theories that underlie the true issues.
- Learn the ins and outs of prevention techniques for any group of learners.
- Understand key approaches and methodology for all encompassing gang prevention and suppression. Benefit from case studies and lessons learned.

So how does the United States defeat this danger called gangs? The Federal Emergency Management cycle of preparing, responding, recovering, and mitigating comes to mind. The gang cycle has three phases: prevention, intervention, and suppression that we will dive into deeper in the upcoming chapters. The overall goal is to rectify the social imbalance in society and eliminate the chaos gangs create. Society must see the common operating picture and consciously embrace issues of criminologists, policy makers, and criminal justice practitioners who are not receptive to holistic approaches. What sets this gang book apart from the others is our unique experiences and real-world encounters. The authors have over 35 years of combined experience in the field of gang suppression.

1   The Problem

Since the beginning of the new millennium nationwide, criminal street gang numbers have been on the rise. These gangs have wreaked havoc in our communities in every aspect of our way of life. In 2002, gangs in the state of Florida were just starting to really show law enforcement and our society what was in store. Law enforcement had a pretty decent handle overall on combating gang-related crime prior to this time. However, it was around this time that law enforcement everywhere in the nation started to get away from combating criminal street gangs and started battling the terrorist threat. September 11, 2001 is a date that in many Americans, minds was just as memorable as Pearl Harbor day was to the previous generation. It was on this day that gangs nationwide started to breathe a sigh of relief. Around the nation, dedicated Gang Units were transformed overnight to Joint Terrorist Task Forces and Anti-Terrorism Units. Numerous law enforcement personnel who had served in the military prior to this time were recalled to fight once again. The result of this was that the nation's gangs got a short-term free pass, so to say. Long-term investigations from R.I.C.O.'s were delayed, and/or forgotten and left by the wayside in order to fight this new threat.

Gangs since this time have been on the rise and are not showing any signs of slowing down. According to the 2011 National Gang Threat Assessment report, gangs are responsible for an average of 48% of violent crime in most jurisdictions, and up to 90% in others. The F.B.I. believes that gang membership is estimated to be over 1.5 million members nationwide and within the last decade, numerous jurisdictions have reported a marked increase in both adult gang participation and female gang participation. Currently, females pose the greatest growing segment of gangs overall nationwide.

In truth, gangs have been around since the beginning of time and will be a dark side of most communities in the distant future. Law enforcement, community outreach programs, and social worker groups from state to state have not been able to combat the threat in any meaningful ways that can be proven. From prevention to suppression and intervention, currently there seems to be no real answer as to how to overcome these criminal groups.

In today's world, gang violence climbs to all-time highs. The increasing number of crimes resulting from gangs are not just a problem here in the United States but worldwide. Currently, gang-related murders are skyrocketing in El Salvador as well as in Honduras and Guatemala (often referred to as the "Northern Triangle"). There, gangs clash in gun fights daily with law enforcement and the homicide rates soar due to gang-related homicide. To those people who do not believe that these problems in the countries to the south are tomorrow's problems for law enforcement here, think again. Gang members from these and many other countries make their way to the United States daily as the border continues to see illegal immigrants crossing with little resistance. These aren't just women and children crossing the border gentle reader, but rather hardcore gang members and drug cartel members as well, are among the thousands of people that cross daily.

Florida is no exception to the gang threat. Florida was coined "the retirement capital of the world" by CNN several years ago and it maintains that laid back, beautiful, sunny beaches, and relaxing atmosphere image currently. Additionally, Florida is well known as a vacation destination for people across the nation and Europeans as well. From spring break students hoping to have the time of their lives, to families visiting Mickey Mouse in Disney World in Orlando, to retirees looking to spend the golden years in the sun and in peace, Florida is believed to be one of the most desirable locations to visit and/or live among all 50 states. What most don't realize is that these same attractions bring with them some of the worst criminal elements across the globe. As we write this book, Florida is currently the fourth most populous state in the nation, with many people coming each new day to try and make a new home and a fresh start for themselves here. Obviously this would include gang members. However, what most people don't realize about Florida is that in 2014 it contained 11 of the top 100 most violent and dangerous cities across the nation. This is more than any other state including California (that has 10 cities), Texas (with 5 cities), and New York (with only 4 cities) (Source is the Huffpost.com "11 of the nation's 100 most dangerous cities are in Florida," Jan 3 2014). It is because of facts like this that Florida is often referred to as the "Gunshine State" by the criminal element and gang members alike. In 2009, an F.B.I. report came out stating that violent street gangs were to blame for up to 80% of the nation's violent crime. If this report is correct and Florida recently had more violent cities than any other state in the union, then these facts could lead one to infer that per population, Florida may have more gang members than any other state.

Al Capone is one of America's most well-known historical gangsters of all time. What some people never knew is that like many, he too had a home in Florida. If you think he only came down to enjoy the sun, you would be gravely wrong. The same is true of many of the nation's worst criminal gang members. What they don't know prior to coming though is that Florida is like no other state in the nation when it comes to gangs. From traditional gangs such as the Bloods of the United Blood Nation and skinheads, to the nontraditional gangs such as "Grand Park" or the "Island Boy Cartel," the gang world here in Florida is a little unlike anywhere else in the world.

In 2008, Plonczynski spoke to a high-ranking member of the Latin Kings in Bradenton, Florida. He asked him why the "Kings" across Florida didn't seem to be as organized as they appeared to be in Chicago or New York. He looked at me and said that Florida was often referred to as the "ghost state." Not just by the Latin Kings but by numerous other gangs as well. He went on to say that rules that traditionally were followed in other states didn't seem to work among many of the gangs here in Florida. This Latin King stated that while he was in prison here in Florida, that he had spoken to numerous other high-ranking members of criminal gangs on this very topic and none of them quite had an answer for it. It wasn't the lack of leadership or anything that they could hang their hat on, but rather some things just didn't work everywhere, such as Florida. The same may be said in Florida's approach to combat the problem. While some programs appear to work in other states, they haven't been attempted here or simply haven't been successful.

The following chapters will show law enforcement's problems with gangs in Florida with some national perspective and how they have attempted to deal with the gang problem on different levels. From the early involvements and beginnings of some of the worst gang members in the state of Florida, this book will show the side of gangs that most never see or even read about. As gang investigators we have been blessed (mostly to still be alive) to see some of the most violent and the worst of what criminal gangs have had to offer.

2 National Perspective

Philadelphia

To offer a different geographical perspective Brzenchek spoke to Captain Xavier Beaufort, a twenty-two-year veteran of the Philadelphia Prison System and someone who has lived in Philadelphia all his life, and has a different perspective on gangs. Captain Beaufort stated that, "Philadelphia has a neighborhood problem, it's more territorial and about protecting their neighborhoods and not a gang problem." When probed more about this statement he went on to say,

> when gangs attempt to settle in various areas the local neighborhood groups run them out of town. Philadelphians won't stand for outside gangs setting up operations taking away from their current enterprise. Whether you're inside or outside Curran-Fromhold the neighborhood groups stay together and when outnumbered rival neighborhoods band together if they are in minority for protection.

What perplexed Brzenchek when he first moved to Philadelphia in 2013 from Washington, DC where he was a police officer under Commissioner Ramsey is the lack of acceptance in formally recognizing a gang issue in Philadelphia. For example, where Captain Beaufort works they are just now implementing a gang intelligence unit after resistance for years and when Brzenchek participated in a ride along in Kensington (coined Heroin Capital of the East Coast by Drugs, Inc.) he requested to ride with the Gang Unit at the Philadelphia Police Department in 2014. Brzenchek was informed by a PPD Official that the Philadelphia Police Department has a Drug Strike Task Force that handles neighborhood-related issues, not a Gang Unit.

Brzenchek worked with A. Benjamin Mannes, CPP, CESP on the Washington DC Metropolitan Police Department and requested Pieper provide an expert comparison of the gang threat in different American cities he has had experience in. Pieper has accomplished so much and has made such an impact in the challenged sixth police district which serves the impoverished, high-crime Anacostia section of Southeast DC: his insight throughout this chapter is invaluable to augment perspectives drawn from Florida that Plonczynski and Peiper have provided.

To give you some context on the tremendous background on Mannes: he serves as the Director of the Office of Investigations at the American Board of Internal Medicine in Philadelphia, PA, where he also serves on the board of InfraGard, the F.B.I.-coordinated public/private partnership, the Peirce College Criminal Justice Advisory Board, and as a leading subject matter expert in exam integrity investigations (high-stakes cheating on standardized tests). Mannes grew up with divorced parents in both Los Angeles, CA and New York City from the 1970s to the 1990s before entering the law enforcement profession as a seasonal officer with the Long Beach (NY) Police Department and as an Auxiliary Police Officer with the NYPD while attending John Jay College of Criminal Justice. He then was appointed as an officer with the US Federal Protective Service where he was assigned to the New York Terrorist Trials Operations Command in the 1990s, then to Washington, DC where he served 10 years with the DC Metropolitan Police and US Department of Homeland Security before being appointed in 2008 to his leadership role at the American Board of Internal Medicine. It was in this career and urban upbringing that Mannes witnessed different trends in gang activity and how they varied from the street gangs of Los Angeles, to the rise of MS-13 in the Virginia suburbs of Washington, the "corner crews" of Southeast DC, and how a serious decline in neighborhood gangs in New York led to the rise of organized gangs like the Bloods, Ñetas, and Latin Kings.

Los Angeles

As a youth in Los Angeles in the 1980s, Mannes witnessed the apex of the gang crisis during a time frame starting at the crack explosion and ending with the 1992 Los Angeles Riots. At the time, violent crime was at its highest in our nation's history, and the tactic of "drive-by shootings" was common in many low-income southland areas like South Central LA, Watts, East LA, Compton, and Inglewood. Many LA gangs of this era were considered the grandfathers of the organized gangs seen today, especially with the "franchising" of various Bloods and Crips sets. The Bloods and Crips were descendants of LA's African-American car club gangs of the 1920s and 1930s, when in the late 1960s a small gang called the "Baby Avenues" began referring to their gang as the "Cribs," which is thought to have eventually given rise to the current name of the South Central gang, the Crips. The activities of the Crips originated on high school campuses throughout the Los Angeles area, which included the "East Side Crips," "West Side Crips," "Compton Crips," "Main Street Crips," "Kitchen Crips," "5 Deuce Crips," and the "Rolling 20 Crips." Despite the fact that these gangs embraced the Crip name, they often remained independent and continued to have their own leadership and members (Dunn, 1999).

During the early 1970s, in an effort to protect themselves from the many Crip gangs forming in the area, the Bloods formed as the "Compton Pirus" and joined forces with the "Laurdes Park Hustlers" and the "LA Brims." Various other gangs around the area who had been attacked or threatened in the past by the Crips later joined the forces against them, and these gangs were united under the Blood name (Dunn, 1999) (Figure 2.1).

Figure 2.1 Latin King Tattoo.

Close to 30,000 gang members associated with either the Crips or Bloods made their home in and around Los Angeles during the early 1980s. Subsequently, and in contrast to biker gangs, most of these Crips and Bloods subsets were in conflict with one another due to the independent nature of several of these gangs.

Like in most other cities, gangs in Los Angeles were racially divided. While the Bloods and Crips wore colors to self-identify (red or blue), the navigation of predominantly Mexican neighborhoods proved more confusing. There are about 500 Hispanic gangs in Los Angeles County, which represents approximately half of the area's gang membership. All Los Angeles Hispanic gangs along with gangs in other Southern California cities are commonly referred to as "South Siders."

Like the neighborhood gangs in most other cities, LA's Hispanic gangs were born from neighborhood identity, called "Barrios."

One of the oldest Hispanic gangs in Los Angeles is called Dog Town Rifa, located in the William Mead housing projects that were built in 1942. The gang had actually been in that area since 1890 when it was a multi-racial group of Irish immigrants, Mexicans, and other ethnic groups that lived in the Chinatown area north of downtown Los Angeles. Other old Hispanic barrios include Temple Street, White Fence in Boyle Heights, 38th Street in South LA, Canta Ranas in Santa Fe Springs, Canoga Park Alabama and San Fers in the San Fernando Valley, Clanton, Florencia, El Hoyo Maravilla, Artesia, Hawaiian Gardens, Dog Patch, and Big Hazard. These gangs are geographically dispersed and not concentrated in one section of Los Angeles they have significant numbers in the San Fernando Valley, San Gabriel Valley, the Beach communities, Long Beach, Compton, and South Los Angeles.

Enforcement

According to Hopper (1987), the gangs epidemic in Los Angeles hit its crescendo in the late 1980s through the early 1990s when the national spotlight came in the form of news coverage, the film "Colors", and gang violence during the 1992 LA Riots. The Los Angeles Police Department (LAPD) and Los Angeles County Sheriffs (LASD) had dedicated gang enforcement units which, while controversial, proved effective in controlling the epidemic.

The LAPD's gang enforcement unit was called Community Resources Against Street Hoodlums (CRASH), which was established by LAPD chief Daryl Gates to combat the rising problem of gangs in Los Angeles, California. Each of the LAPD's 18 divisions had a CRASH unit assigned to it, whose primary goal was to suppress the influx of gang-related crimes in Los Angeles. However, CRASH's success could be less attributed to street enforcement and more in the intelligence gathering and sharing. In addition to gang-related crime prevention, CRASH officers were assigned specific gangs within their division to obtain intelligence on, which they relayed to detectives and between divisions. A great example of CRASH was when, in 1987, Chief Daryl Gates initiated "Operation Hammer." As a result of increasing gang violence and a drive-by killing resulting in the death of seven people, Chief Gates responded by sending CRASH officers to arrest suspected gang members. At the height of this operation in April 1988, 1,453 people were arrested by 1,000 police officers in *a single weekend.*

Similar to CRASH, the LASD had "Operation Safe Streets" (OSS), which was different from CRASH as it had less than half of their manpower, but all were assigned to plain clothes in an intelligence and investigative capacity. The OSS model for gang intelligence was adapted nationwide, mainly because the LASD not only had policing responsibilities for most of the unincorporated jurisdictions within LA County, but also oversaw the LA County Jail. LASD OSS became known for their ability to develop reliable gang informants, as intelligence is the key to any successful anti-gang operation. This was enhanced and supported by fellow deputies working in the county jail. The county jail would later form its own Gang Unit modeled after OSS calling it Operation Safe Jails (OSJ). Further analysis in comparison to the New York City Corrections Gang Intelligence unit proved the value of a correctional component to gang enforcement, building upon the LASD model.

Lastly, the professionalization and growth of the Los Angeles School Police Department (LASPD) is worth mentioning when studying the enforcement of the LA gang problem. In the 1980s, LA Unified Schools were considered incubators of violent street gangs. While cities like New York and Philadelphia continued to have unarmed security guards with no arrest authority or investigative capabilities policing their schools, LASPD had the largest independent school police department in the United States, with over 410 sworn police officers, 101 non-sworn school safety officers (SSO), and 34 civilian support staff, including a full-service investigative division, and critical response team. While recent superintendents have claimed that the LASPD is not sharing school records with gang intelligence databases, it is clear that the deployment of a professionally certified, full service police agency to provide liaison with municipal and county law enforcement has positively impacted the gang problem and promoted safety in schools.

New York

New York, as America's largest city, is an extremely good place to look when analyzing the cyclical evolution of gang crime. Gangs are part of the rich and storied history of New York, with numerous street gangs vying for territory in the various neighborhoods and cultural subsets of the city. When I was a youth, gangs were normally broken down by neighborhood, and could be identified racially (there were gangs of every race and ethnicity) and with their attire. Like the biker gangs of the 1960s and 1970s, NYC street gangs of that era wore "cuts," which were leather or denim vests or jackets with their club name/logo on the back. These neighborhood crews were the norm, but in the violent era of the 1970s and 1980s, leading up to the crack explosion, NYC gangs became more organized and followed more national trends, to include the territorial position of the following organized gangs:

The Latin Kings, more formally known as the Almighty Latin King and Queen Nation is a large Hispanic street gang based largely in New York and Chicago, with territories in Puerto Rican, Dominican, and Mexican communities. While the gang originally dates back to Chicago in 1954, the Bloodline Manifesto was founded by Luis Felipe AKA "King Blood" in 1986 in the Collins State Correctional Facility in New York. New York/Bloodline Latin Kings identify as the "Almighty Latin King and Queen Nation (ALKQN)." Membership is estimated to be as many as 7,500, divided among several dozen tribes operating in 15 cities in 5 states. In New York City, the Latin Kings are organized into individual "tribes." These tribes are located throughout the five boroughs and Long Island (Figure 2.2).

Figure 2.2 Pieper with Blood Graffiti.

From 1986 to the internal power struggle that erupted in 1994, the ALKQN solid-ified its role as a gang through crimes such as murder, racketeering, and R.I.C.O. Act charges. In 1991, ALKQN members numbered about 2,000, both incarcer-ated and free. In 1994, with the rapid growth of the Latin Kings, an internal power struggle erupted and violence within the Kings ensued. Between June 1993 and February 1994, seven Latin Kings were murdered. Following the outbreaks of internal gang violence, Luis Felipe and 19 others were charged with murder and racketeering; the indictments ended in 1995 with 39 Latin Kings and one Latin Queen indicted under the R.I.C.O. Act (Brotherton, 2004). The year 1999 was believed to be the beginning of the ALKQN's transformation from a street gang to a "street organization." At this time, Latin Kings and their female counter-parts, the Latin Queens, began appearing *en masse* at political demonstrations in support of the Latino community. To further its transformation and efforts to legitimize, the organization began to hold its monthly meetings (called universals) at St. Mary's Episcopal Church in West Harlem. At this time, the membership of the Latin Kings is believed to have swelled to 3,000 incarcerated and 4,000 free. The monthly universals drew attendance of 500–600 regularly. Internal changes to the organization began to take place as Fernandez amended the ALKQN manifesto to include parliamentary elections and new procedures for handling inter-organizational grievances and removing death as a possible punishment, replacing it with "vanishing," the act of being banished from the movement.

This transformation got the attention of the F.B.I. as well, who started making R.I.C.O. cases on the Latin Kings. In 1997, their leader was sentenced to the harshest penalty passed down for a federal crime since World War II, 250 years in prison, with the first 45 to be spent in solitary confinement. Another 39 members were sentenced to an average of 20 years in prison for their roles in the crimes. The year would bring further legal troubles as 32 others were arrested in a raid in the Lower East Side and charged with disorderly conduct. The Special Commissioner of Investigation for Schools soon after charged the ALKQN with infiltrating the school system; a school security guard with 5 years of service was dismissed on charges of unprofessional conduct for his association with the Latin Kings (Brotherton, 2004).

In 1998, a joint operation of the F.B.I., New York City Police Department (NYPD), Immigration and Naturalization Service (INS), New York State Police, and the Drug Enforcement Administration (DEA) came to a close with the arrests of 92 suspected ALKQN members. The Latin King leadership insisted over half of those arrested were not members. The operation, dubbed Operation Crown, cost the city over $1,000,000 and took 19 months to complete.

The Ñetas represent the other powerhouse in the Latino community. The Ñetas are a gang that began in the Puerto Rican prison system and spread to the United States. Although Puerto Rico has hundreds of small street gangs claiming its poorer neighborhoods, Ñetas is by far the largest and most dominant, controlling the illegal drug trade on the island. The gang claims about 15,000 members in Puerto Rico, 10,000 in the United States, and nearly 10,000 in other parts of the world. In 2009 they were reported as having up to 6,000 members in the North East Coast of the U.S. alone and up to almost 13,000 in South America and thousands more worldwide. The Ñetas mainly operate out of the tri-state and upstate area, although they have ties with Los Sangeros Nuestra Familia, a mob family that operates in Puerto Rico; the leader of the mob family is El Don. In New York, they have founding chapters in Kings County, Queens County, Nassau County, Suffolk County, Montgomery County, Oneida County, Otsego County, and Monroe County. They also have strong legions throughout the New Jersey area including Hudson County, Passaic County, and Essex County and are known to have over more than 30 chapters in New Jersey alone.

On June 3, 2003, seven leaders of the Ñeta Association were arrested in Long Island, New York, for the stabbing and murder of two MS-13 members. On May 6, 2009, a Ñeta drug den was discovered and busted by the Drug Enforcement Administration, in the Queensbridge Housing Projects, located in Long Island City, Queens. 156 kilograms of cocaine and 487 pounds of marijuana were found in the apartment complex located on 41st Street and Vernon Blvd. In 2009, the Ñetas were reported to have major conflict with former allies, the Bloods, and a more severe conflict with the Salvadorian MS-13 gang. In 2010, reports said the Ñetas had been seen operating and connecting with the Bloods and Latin Kings. Ñetas are still having conflict and dangerous altercations with the Salvadorian MS-13 gang and the "Dominicans Don't Play" gang (DDP). In 2014 the Ñetas reached a peace treaty with almost if not all who claimed enemy to them. In many parts of not just the United States but other countries the Ñetas are rebuilding their image by becoming more involved in communities and politics (Navarro, 1997).

In the early 1990s, **the Bloods and Crips** started to appear in New York, despite their roots as a West Coast street gang, with the Bloods being more prominent. According to gang experts Ron "Cook" Barrett and Kevin Deutsch, West Coast gangs have started organizing inside correctional facilities and then take hold on the streets following the release of their members. Traditionally, since 1993, the Bloods have been the power within Rikers Island and many state correctional facilities. Sets like the Mac Ballers, G Shine, Brims, and Gorilla Brims have been active and constantly fighting for control of facilities. They outnumber many rivals. There are Crip sets, Latin Kings, Trinitarios, Gangster Disciples, MS-13, and others active.

Every nationality is represented within the gang culture and with the African-American population in New York State prisons being the largest, the gangs will reflect that. In California, for example, because of the Mexican population, the Mexican Mafia (Sureños, Nuestra Familia) are the power groups. With the Hispanic population growing in New York State, these groups are starting to become more visible in the state. The largest ethnic group in the area will dictate what type of gangs you see (Ferranti, 2015) (Figure 2.3).

Figure 2.3 MS-13 Graffiti.

According to experts, the Bloods and Crips are likely the largest gangs in the region, with each boasting dozens of sets across the five boroughs and Long Island. The Bloods currently appear to have more members, due to especially high membership rates in and around low-income housing projects in the Bronx, Brooklyn, and Queens, as well as on Rikers Island. The Bloods boast higher membership numbers largely because of their decades-old presence in impoverished pockets of the city—areas that have withstood several waves of gentrification. The staying power of many local Bloods sets—despite scores of gang sweeps and crackdowns over the years—has been remarkable. Collectively, however, the number of young men belonging to independent neighborhood cliques and crews still outnumber Bloods and Crips. They are so abundant, and densely spread across the region, that it's difficult to say which of them is the largest in terms of membership (Commission, 2015).

Enforcement

Like in Los Angeles, the NYPD has established specific units, which emphasize reducing gang-related criminal activity in the city. However, the most innovative example of gang enforcement comes from the model of the LA County Sheriffs, not the LAPD. In an effort to combat this growing gang presence in NYC jails, to include the massive Rikers Island complex, an interdepartmental Gang Task Force between the NYPD and NYC Corrections Department, an agency that unlike many prisons agencies in America carries full state peace officer status, was formed in 1994. The purpose of the task force was to assess the nature of gang activity within correctional facilities, review gang management practices and procedures within the department as well as in comparative correctional facilities, and to develop recommendations for the promulgation of a DOC-wide policy on gangs. In 1995, this task force took correctional investigators outside their respective facilities and onto joint investigations with the police. In March 1997, the NYC Department of Corrections formed a Gang Intelligence Unit (GIU). Soon after, they installed an enhanced "Superbase" computer program that compiled all of the department's security risk group information into one database. The system was so successful that outside agencies that were made aware of the information began to work with the department to gather intelligence for their own investigations (Domash, 1999).

By 2001, NYC Corrections had 38 armed, sworn detectives, four captains, and a deputy warden assigned to GIU, with matching numbers from the NYPD (Martin, 2010). Not only did the use of corrections investigators mark a shift in gang investigative tactics, but it also helped levy charges on both sides of the "wall." Shortly after Commissioner Bernard Kerik started the Total Efficiency Accountability Management System (TEAMS) at the NYC Corrections Department, corrections investigators started working with the District Attorney's offices to charge inmates with crimes committed in jail, as opposed to just administrative punishments like solitary confinement. This program, in combination with the

GIU, assured that gang members inside and outside the correctional system can be charged with criminal conspiracies, a necessary element to breaking up gang leadership structures.

Washington, DC

It is often said that gangs represent an urban microcosm reflective of the cities they operate in, and Washington, DC is no exception. While most Americans who have never lived in DC commonly believe, based on the fact that it's the capital city of the most powerful nation in the world, that the extensive law enforcement community there is organized and systematic in their approach to gang interdiction, organized crime, and public safety. Unfortunately, this is not true. Meanwhile, upon my appointment to the DC Metropolitan Police Department (MPD) and assignment to the notorious Anacostia section of Southeast DC in the late 1990s, the gangs of DC were far from organized, consisting of a patchwork of neighborhood "corner crews." As of 2009, there were over 120 gangs in operation throughout the 28-square-mile district, normally based on a neighborhood and high school as a geographic boundary (King, 2009).

Furthermore, during my tenure at MPD, Chief Charles Ramsey and later his protégé, Cathy Lanier, shifted the focus of policing strategies from traditional uniformed response and investigations to one of increased visibility versus specialized response. This meant that the vast majority of the department was shifted to high-visibility patrol service areas with specialized units being shifted to patrol redeployment at least one week a month, leaving little manpower for specialized intelligence or investigative duties. This meant that until his retirement from the department, there was only one first-grade detective, Neil Trugman (now a commander with the Amtrak Police), assigned to gang intelligence and high-level investigation in the city, with only a handful available to assist him at any given time. Add this MPD deployment schema to the fact that there was no school district police and the closing of Lorton Prison, which meant the DC Corrections Department had no Gang Intelligence Unit and was farming prisoners out to the Federal Bureau of Prisons; DC had little capability to track gang activity in comparison to the other aforementioned major American cities.

Then, from south of the Potomac River in the early 2000s, a new organized gang threat emerged. At the time, a new wave of Salvadorian, Ecuadorian, and Peruvian immigrants were settling in Virginia's Fairfax and Prince William counties. As the DC Metro area is a sprawling patchwork of suburban counties spread out on either side of the District of Columbia across Virginia and Maryland; immigration settlement is not fixed to certain neighborhoods as it is in older, more established communities of immigration. Therefore, the police and social services sectors in the DC area were ill-equipped with the language skills and requisite knowledge of where these immigrants originated, in comparison to places like New York, LA, Chicago, or Miami. Because of this, the Central American communities of Fairfax and Prince William County, Virginia, and later Montgomery

Figure 2.4 Female MS-13 Gang Member.

and Prince George's County, Maryland became overrun by the Salvadorian MS-13 gang. By the late 2000s, MS-13 had organized itself as the preeminent drug importer in these communities and as the Hispanic communities in DC's Georgia Ave and Columbia Road corridors started to grow, MS-13 moved into the district and set up shop, creating a violent shockwave to the unorganized DC gang landscape. By 2014, when a wave of Central American youths started surging across the US border to flee violent gangs in their home countries, those arriving in DC were rapidly being recruited by a growing, more powerful MS-13 (Birr, 2016) (Figure 2.4).

Enforcement

Based on the interjurisdictional nature of policing in the DC area, federal law enforcement agencies have taken the primary investigative lead into the MS-13 gang, as well as prior R.I.C.O. cases targeted at crack and heroin distribution through DC's "Corner Crews" (to include the notable case against DC drug kingpin Rayful Edmond in 1989). This proves an issue because gang cases of this nature often take the observations of local law enforcement to get the initial evidence and link analysis necessary to escalate a case to a R.I.C.O. indictment, in addition to the fact that all gang-related violence is initially investigated by the catching local law enforcement agency.

A good example of this comes from an uptick in MS-13-related homicides throughout the DC area in 2015–2016, when eight murders were attributed to them. The recent uptick in violence can be traced to a failed gang truce in El Salvador and the aforementioned surge of unaccompanied Central American children who entered the United States in the same time period. In one of the eight killings with MS-13 ties, three young men were charged in connection with the fatal shooting of a 17-year-old in rural Loudoun County, Virginia, which is settled in the hills between Dulles Airport and the West Virginia border. The perpetrators and victims were identified as having entered the United States illegally in 2013 as unaccompanied children who later skipped immigration hearings.

At the same time as the Loudoun County murder, a large trial of MS-13 members in Northern Virginia took place, with 13 men facing charges related to three killings and attempted murder of people who either left the gang, stood up to its members, or were suspected of providing information about the gang's activities to law enforcement.

However, in the mid-2000s Maryland prosecutors oversaw a series of cases that resulted in prison sentences for dozens of high-level gang leaders, to where Montgomery County State's Attorney John McCarthy said they "did effectively cut the head off the gang." Therefore, as MS-13 is organized and effectively based outside the borders of the United States, once a group is indicted and taken off the streets, new leadership is selected and the recruitment from the immigrant community continues, with drug trafficking and prostitution being conducted to fund operations.

3   Discussion

As the world changes the criminal justice system needs to be altered to meet those societal needs and some kind of criminal justice reform introduced to keep abreast of these changes (Kuhn, 1996). There are many instances in which the reforms or initiatives taken by the criminal justice system fail to accomplish what they were intended for. Some see this failure in criminal justice reform as a result of not having an effective evaluation system in place and low levels of accountability (Middendorf, 2013). Often there is a change in policy, new programs are introduced, training is provided, but the same evaluation system is used. Stronge and Tucker (2003) believed that a conceptually sound and a properly implemented evaluation system are vital components for reform efforts (Figure 3.1).

Figure 3.1 Sur 13 Threatens Rival Gang.

4 Criminal Justice Transformation

Criminal justice transformation is based on the premise that both "criminal justice and learning" are ways and reasons for creating a society in which human potentials are realized (Ahmed, 2010, p. 516). Uys (2007) stated that managing change can be challenging but pertaining to criminal justice it is necessary to meet the needs of a changing society. According to Jorgensen (2005), there is a challenge in finding ways to address issues faced by at-risk youths. Reaction to change in criminal justice will vary, depending on the levels of acceptance by stakeholders. Transformation in criminal justice can be advantageous as long as the results are positive (Uys, 2007).

Changes and new trends in the criminal justice system led to criminal justice transformation; this involves the creation of new programs, policies, and revamping old criminal justice programs (Jorgensen, 2005). Gang prevention programs were introduced as part of recent criminal justice reform to address disparities among the different groups. Transformations in criminal justice will continue for years to come and this will require the transformation of programs for them to remain relevant. There is evidence of success in using this program to address criminal justice reform initiatives, but meticulous implementation and sustainability will be necessary. Programs create a new institutional culture which is important in institutional growth and development, but the influence on culture can cause repercussions if they are not properly managed.

The Role of Leaders in Criminal Justice Reform

The role of leaders in criminal justice reform cannot be over emphasized; it can impact the organizational structure and influence change. When criminal justice leaders are aware of their roles and what is expected of them, they are able to make better choices (Schechter, 2012). According to Gadeken (2012), leaders should focus on building leadership capacity and offering support for new and struggling staff to help them to achieve their maximum potential. Building leadership teams will not only help to increase the skills as leaders but also better the environment they lead in (Loertscher, 2008a). It is crucial for leaders to use their expertise and experience to build knowledge base and boost programs (Loertscher, 2005). In doing this it is important to provide adequate professional assistance through regular staff development sessions, including external workshops or bringing in resource persons. Ensure that all the available resources are utilized to maximize the effectiveness of these programs (DuFour, DuFour, & Eaker, 2008).

Accountability

In reviewing and sharing the information gathered in PGPs, leaders would be able to plan for and work on areas that appear to be weak as well as maintain strength. Understanding data and sharing the results with parents will give a better understanding of performance and assure them that the staff is working on maintaining or improving crime rates. Sharing results also helps to build community relations and trust (Loertscher, 2005). Leaders should be prepared for eventualities; ensuring expectations for themselves and their staff and ensure they live up to the expectations of their job. Encourage sharing of mental learning from each other (Sajeva, 2007). Planning for developing gang prevention programs and identifying needs and providing for them are some of the ways of ensuring success. Thigpen (2011) emphasized that criminal justice leaders should have "knowledge to reform" as well as the "knowledge of the dynamics of change" (p. 2). This knowledge is likely to help these leaders effectively implement and maintain programs (Thigpen, 2011).

Criminal Justice Organizations

Programs are implemented at all levels of the criminal justice system and some may use gang prevention (Hodges, 2003). The underlining components of programs in all these criminal justice institutions are collaboration and achievement (Hughes-Hassell, Brasfield, & Dupree, 2012). Each level may appear different depending on the organization (Spanneut, 2010). As they prepare to face the challenges that come with entering the profession for the first time, new gang investigators can benefit from participating in predictive gang prevention programs as they can learn from more experienced gang investigators in their community (Lovett & Cameron, 2011).

Criminal justice leaders can reshape an unethical organizational culture by being a role model for employees (Costa, 2013). It is important that leaders practice what they preach by instilling the correct values in employees and ensuring that their actions are ethical as well. Burgess, Newton, and Riveros (2012) posited that constant communication between leaders and employees is crucial; leaders need to remind employees of ethical principles through memos, newsletters, bulletins, and other media. According to Donaldson (1992) there should be constant professional development activities and refresher courses regarding "code of ethics, code of conduct, sexual discrimination/harassment, human welfare, rights, duties, responsibilities, and social contracts" that are made available and in most cases mandatory for employees to participate in.

According to Jones (2010), unethical behavior occurs as a result of self-interest. It is therefore crucial for organizations to focus on the employees' interest collectively. Transformational leaders encourage open, honest, and timely communication, and foster dialogue and collaboration between team members (Amar, Hentrich, & Hlupic, 2009). In transforming an organization, leaders need to also transform the culture of the organization; this may require modification to the organization's vision and mission to incorporate the ethical principles that will improve the organization (Jones, 2010). There should also be a system of reward for upholding ethical behaviors and consequences for breaking them. An example of a reward could be verbal or written recognition for departments that consistently uphold the ethical culture of keeping students' data confidential and promoting ethical principles.

5   Gang Trends

Let's take a look at a growing trend that is moving not only up and down Florida but throughout the U.S. Our "old" traditional gangs such as the Black Gangster Disciple Nation (BGDN), Vice Lords, Bloods, and Crips have transformed into much different gangs than they were just 20 years ago. Back in the day, many of these gangs had just one overall leader like Larry Hoover, Willy Lloyd, and Jeff Fort. The Bloods and Crips have always had "set" leaders and not so much just one overall leader; maybe with the exception of Stanley "Tookie" Williams and Raymond Lee Washington. Since the incarceration or death of such subjects, the gangs have broken up into many small sets and cliques. Due to the high-ranking leadership not being around for one reason or another, there is fighting and unrest within the gang; this has been happening with the Bloods and Crips almost since their beginning, but it was different for other gangs. As the years have passed and law enforcement has continued to track and combat them, they have evolved. The BGDN has broken into too many sets to count, to include Brothers of the Strong Struggle (BOSS), Insane Gangster Disciple (IGD), Gangster Discipline and Folk. The point I'm trying to make is that gangs and gang members have evolved. If there is a major national gang name attached to a local gang's name it has little to no identification with the original gang such as the East Side Goonie Goon Bloods in Bradenton, FL. They wore red and represented to the right as do many Blood sets in an attempt to pay homage back to the West Coast but other than that, they were nothing like the Bloods of the olden days. In today's world, many of the gangs we're dealing with have names such as 3rd Shift, Mutt Crew, 41 Boyz, and Show Off. Many times, these gangs have a name that relates to a specific street, neighborhood, or housing development, or they call themselves a "rap group."

As time has gone on and the mainstream media has glorified the gangster culture, major celebrities have aligned themselves with gangs and true homegrown gang members have gotten celebrity status. The unfortunate part of this is that today's youth seldom see the problems in the movies, TV programs, or music as real. As kids, we don't understand the true meaning of why Miley Cyrus is wearing all red and black in a video for a song called "23." The reality is that there were known members of the Bloods gang in that video, they used Blood hand signs and Blood handshakes. We are just using this as an example, by no means are we saying that Miley Cyrus is a Blood gang member, but at a minimum she was/is associating with them. Mainstream rappers such as Lil Wayne make it very clear that they are Blood gang members and do not hide their affiliation.

This evolution of gangs and gangsters has created a bit of a problem for law enforcement. On the one hand, the youth of today see these gang members making a ton of money and getting very famous doing it. Rarely do they see the flip side of things where law enforcement is raiding their house and taking everything that they own because, in addition to rapping they were also trafficking in large amounts of narcotics. Kids today are more likely to be involved in this culture if they feel that there are no repercussions for their actions.

In this portion of the book, we are going to take a look at how law enforcement can work cases on local or "hybrid" gangs who want to call themselves "rap groups," and then follow the evolution of gangs as they have gone from generation to generation and changed their names several times. Rappers such as Snoop Dogg and Lil Wayne have been very proud of their gang affiliation to the Bloods and Crips for decades. At this point in their careers, it's going to be pretty hard to work a case against them or use their music against them. What is meant by that is that ever since the beginning of rap music, rappers have maintained that they sing about what they see in their everyday lives. They have sung about real-life incidents and events that have occurred to them. Several years ago, Snoop was facing murder charges and he came out with a song called "Murder Was the Case." As time has gone on, he still lets everyone in the world know that he is a Crip, but it has been harder to place him next to the gang as an actual member who is "putting in work" out on the streets. When law enforcement deals with gang members at an early age or early on in their rap careers, it is easier for law enforcement to take action and use their songs to prove their stories as true.

One example of this would be a case that Pieper worked against a 3rd Shift gang member. On April 12, 2008, Pieper was working a special detail with the Tampa Bay area Multi Agency Gang Taskforce (MAGTF). They had the task force in Bradenton assist us with saturation in known gang areas. They would do these operations from time to time and always had great success. They never had less than 20 arrests on any of these operations and seized large amounts of money, narcotics, and cars. Well, at about 2:00 pm, some task force officers spotted a subject later identified as Darnel Washington AKA Murda driving his vehicle and ran a stop sign at the intersection of 3rd St West and MLK BLVD. The officers initiated a traffic stop. Murda continued to drive for about four blocks before he finally pulled over. When the officers walked up to the car Murda had marijuana all over his shirt and shorts, small bags of powder cocaine in plain view on the front passenger seat, and a vial of "rock" cocaine on the front passenger seat as well.

Come to find out, Murda was packaging his product as he was driving and making deliveries. Needless to say, he was not a very experienced drug dealer. Upon searching the vehicle and securing all of the evidence, Pieper looked at his case of CDs. Florida State Statute 874.08 allows law enforcement to seize any profits, proceeds, and instrumentalities of criminal street gang involvement, meaning that if law enforcement locates any shirts, pictures (with gang members flashing gang hand signs), bandannas, or CDs with a rap group or gang name on it, they can seize it. This statute is very similar to narcotics paraphernalia; however, it's not illegal. They can seize it, place it into evidence, and use it come sentencing time.

As Pieper was looking through Murda's CDs, he noticed that one had "3rd Shift" written on it. Pieper asked Murda if he was a rapper, and he said yes. Pieper then asked him if he rapped with "3rd Shift." Murda stated that he did and that he was on the CD that Pieper had located in the vehicle. Murda was taken back to the command post where Pieper read him his Miranda rights. Post-Miranda, Murda stated that he was indeed packaging his narcotics while he was driving and that's why he didn't see the stop sign that he failed to stop at. Murda and Pieper then listened to a few of the tracks that were on Murda's CD that was located in the vehicle. In one song called "Gangster Bop," Murda has a line where he talks about his gang affiliation, their name, and the color of their bandanna. "Third Shift Murda baby, gangster walkin gangster boppin. Third Shift thuggin, got my black bandanna on," said Murda in one verse. It was clear from the voice in the CD compared to the one in the post-Miranda interview that it was Murda singing. Later on in the song, Murda talks about selling drugs as well. Pieper played the song for the jury and judge during the trial. As a first-time offender, Murda received an 18-month prison sentence and is now a convicted felon. In fact, after that case, Plonczynski and his agency were able to use many of the seized 3rd Shift CDs to work a State and Federal R.I.C.O. case on 3rd Shift sending many gang members away for very long periods of time.

This is just one example of how law enforcement can use the gang's early songs against them. In other songs local rappers have talked about drive-by shootings that they have committed on the mothers of their rival gang members. Pieper and Plonczynski have used these songs and the corresponding police reports against these gang members in criminal cases. These cases can be very easy and beneficial if the gang and their actions are documented properly. In this case, Murda's lawyer's biggest argument was that her client did not have tattoos which meant that he was/is not a gang member. Once again, if the gang or "rap group" is documented properly, it won't matter and they'll be going away for a decent period of time. Thanks to the evolution of technology, nobody makes CDs anymore… now, there is social networking sights like Facebook, Instagram, and YouTube where gang members are making their own videos and law enforcement now has free audio and video evidence!

When talking about the evolution of gangs over the last 20 years, Pieper thinks the biggest change has been in what law enforcement refers to as "hybrid" gangs. Gangs that have no national affiliation, may or may not use graffiti, don't care about the FOLK or PEOPLE nations, and have no real "colors" to speak of, but they do have a name and commit crime together. As mentioned above, they may call themselves a rap group and pick their name from a street, park, or housing development. This has been a huge problem for law enforcement to keep up-to-date with the documentation on these groups. Back in the late 1970s and 1980s, law enforcement had to convince the justice system and society as a whole that the major national gangs like the Bloods and Crips were not just "wayward youth" who were bored and needed after-school programs. The violence and narcotics use/sale was so ramped that people could no longer turn a blind eye.

Fast forward 20 years, now we have to educate people that today's gang members are no longer wearing only red or blue. They still commit the same crimes and are just as violent, but they wear tight "skinny" jeans and T-shirts. In this next section, Pieper is going to take you through generations of gangs that called themselves "rap groups" and how they changed the gangster culture in Manatee County.

When Pieper first got hired by the Bradenton Police Department in 2003 and began field training, he would often see a minivan driving around town that had a local rapper's name on it along with his label and rap group's name. It had I.B.C. in big bold letters on the side for Island Boy Cartel. The I.B.C. was a group of about 10 individuals who took their rap careers at least somewhat seriously, another 15–20 subjects who would provide a verse here and there, and then about another 30 associates who just wanted to smoke weed and hang out with the gang, or rap group. This doesn't take into account all of the groupies and tagalongs that were at the concerts and parties too. Some of the members of the I.B.C. were actually decent rappers and made several CDs, and they would perform all over Florida and Georgia. They sold their CDs out of the trunks of their cars along with sacks of weed. They would also hang out on the street corner selling crack and powder cocaine and do drive-by shootings. They had no real colors to speak of, however; camouflage was popular at the time, so they would wear a lot of it and they would get I.B.C. tattooed on them. They also had a hand sign that they would flash to one another.

Pieper began to document the gang by seizing CDs and conducting interviews of the gang members. Pieper began to snag an I.B.C. CD here and talk to a member of the gang there. After a while, Pieper was able to learn that the man who owned the minivan with I.B.C. all over it was known as "Dollar Bill" AKA Shaquan Billings. "Dollar Bill" was about Pieper's age, but instead of taking a football scholarship to college after high school, he began to rap and sell drugs. "Dollar Bill" and several of his fellow I.B.C. members continued to rap and perform for several years. Many of them would frequently get arrested for a variety of crimes including narcotics possession, fleeing to elude or Driving While License Suspended (DWLS), domestic battery, and of course the drive-by shootings and weapons violations as well. As with most gang-related crimes, these cases went unprosecuted, and victims and witnesses refused to cooperate with the state attorney's office. Another strike against law enforcement was that these kids were young, some of them were just beginning their adult criminal careers at the time. The problem with that is that not very many judges want to send such young kids away for long periods of time.

But Pieper and Plonczynski trucked along trying to make the best possible cases that they could. Right around 2006–2007, another rap group popped up, and they called themselves 3rd Shift. They were younger kids ranging in age from 15 to 18 at the time. These kids also rapped and had a hand sign, but they wore black from head to toe and wore black bandannas. 3rd Shift became known as the enforcement arm of the I.B.C. They carried out many of the more violent and dangerous crimes so that the older members of the I.B.C. would be protected from prosecution. In one interview of a 3rd Shift member, Plonczynski and Pieper were told that 3rd Shift got their name because they sold drugs for the I.B.C. in the 3rd or midnight shift.

3rd Shift consisted of about 20 rappers who took their narcotics-selling careers very seriously and enjoyed rapping and performing from time to time when they had some downtime from turning powder cocaine into "cookies" and doing drive-by shootings. 3rd Shift quickly became a huge problem for not just Manatee County, but Pieper and Plonczynski as well. Once again, they had troubl prosecuting 3rd Shift members because people refused to cooperate with the SAO, and since many 3rd Shift members were juveniles, they were in and out of the system at a rapid rate. Every now and again, Pieper and Plonczynski would get lucky and be able to have the juvenile judge send a member to a 6- to 9-month program.

So now, there are two totally different gangs that are aligned, working in conjunction with one another, and there is a clear hierarchy. Just when it couldn't get any more troublesome, in about 2009, another group came around calling themselves the FAM BOIs. These kids were about 14–15 years old and couldn't care less about rapping. The FAM BOIs loved stealing cars. In the summer of 2010, Pieper is pretty sure they stole just about every Chrysler minivan within the city limits of Bradenton. How the FAM BOIs operated was that they would go out and steal cars for the 3rd Shift and in return 3rd Shift would buy the stolen cars from them and supply them with narcotics to sell. All the proceeds from all the drugs sold by 3rd Shift and the FAM BOIs went straight back to the I.B.C.

As the years strolled along, Plonczynski and his team began to work a state and federal R.I.C.O. on 3rd Shift, and Pieper and his team were able to send many of the FAM BOIs to juvenile programs for stealing cars. At one point just about all of the FAM BOIs were in juvenile programs due to the fact that when they would steal a car and joyride in it they would eventually get caught in the vehicle. Due to their young age they weren't very experienced at fleeing to elude or running from the police. When law enforcement would round all of them up in a stolen vehicle their M.O. was that one of them would take the fall for stealing the vehicle. This worked great (not so much for them) as they eventually ran out of people to take the charge and all of them ended up confessing to stealing a vehicle. In their minds they saw it as if one guy confessed then the police had to let the rest of them go.

Right around the time that Plonczynski and his guys were wrapping up their case on 3rd Shift the FAM BOIs were getting released from their juvenile programs. They had learned that the police had documented the FAM BOIs as a gang, so they changed their name to Pirates Life. The FAM BOIs of old had no hand sign nor did they wear specific colors; however, Pirates Life wore all Pittsburgh Pirates clothing. They had also graduated from stealing cars to very violent armed robberies. Many of the Pirates Life gang members are now serving very long prison terms or getting ready to be tried in federal court for armed robbery.

As things stand today, the I.B.C. still has a few of its original rappers out on the street. Some of them are still slinging dope up on the block and attempting to make it in the rap industry. "Dollar Bill" got federally indicted and is serving 20 years in federal prison. He was popped with four stash houses and over 45 pounds of marijuana. He had also recently signed with a major rap label out of Miami. The youngest generation of all of this mess calls themselves C.O.D. for Choppas On Deck. They do have a hand sign and also hold up their 3s to pay respect to 3rd Shift.

Malls: Ground Zero for Recruitment

Malls have been a center point for communities across the United States for decades. These are places for families and friends to meet and have fun. Teenagers often go to the mall to meet other friends and interact with individuals of the same age.

However, as time progressed, gangs have increased their web of fear on communities across the United States by making these community focal points places of violence and fear. Gang graffiti has increased at malls over the past two decades as well as the violence and number of gang-related shootings at malls. Gangs have learned over the years that law enforcement presence at the malls is often lax and view these types of locations as places where they can conduct business with anonymity and little worry about repercussions to their criminal enterprise.

Moreover, street gangs use local malls as breeding grounds. It is here in our malls that gangs are recruiting, marking their territory, and selling narcotics. Gang members like to go to the mall for almost all the same reasons as good law-abiding citizens do. Gang members like to gather in social places, eat, play video games, watch movies, and look for members of the opposite sex. There is one huge difference—gang members are seldom at the mall to shop or spend money. Gang members do not care about getting the best holiday deals. In the end, gang members at the mall can only lead to bad results for the mall shop owners and the patrons of these stores. With the exception of schools, malls are perhaps the most common place for gang members to meet one another and to encounter rival gangs.

Unfortunately, rival gangs often come in contact with one another at malls as well. When this occurs, violence is usually the outcome. Gang fights have been well documented at malls over the past 5–10 years and seem to be increasing at an alarming rate. In July 2007, a gang-related brawl occurred where approximately 200 teenagers were engaged in a massive fight, forcing authorities to evacuate the mall. This occurred at the Triangle Town Center Mall in Raleigh, North Carolina where there had been few problems prior to this incident. Law enforcement has since come out and said that this fight was instigated by rival gangs fighting.

Gang fights occur on a regular basis at malls across the nation. These fights are often seen as thugs and teenagers acting out by those not willing to take a closer look at the cause or who don't have the proper background to see the real threat behind these fights. In truth, gang fights occur at a more alarming rate than is most likely known or reported. Most of the time, law enforcement is called and show up after the perpetrators have fled; or in other cases, they are not called at all. Either way, reports when these circumstances occur are rare and infrequent due to lack of precise facts of what took place. Likewise, when gang fights like these occur, guns are often present and collateral damage to the civilian population that is present often takes place. This was the case at a local mall several years ago, when members of the violent Sur 13 gang observed rivals of another gang. A fist fight erupted just outside one of the mall exits in broad day light. Moments later, one gang member pulled a handgun and began shooting. One 0.45 caliber round traveled the entire distance of that wing in the mall (approximately 50 yards), going through two partitions until finally stopping in a shop exterior wall. No one was injured, however with malls being well known as hang outs for teenagers, the potential for collateral damage or worse was very much present. This wasn't the only gang altercation that has taken place at that same mall. One year later during the December Christmas rush, two rival gangs had a confrontation in the food court area. This is a place where usually the most numerous mall shoppers can be located. At first, rivals flashed gang hand signs at one another. This quickly led to an exchange of words. Then, as things began to look like a fight was about to occur, one of the gang members pulled out a handgun. The resulting scene was likened to an old west bar with two men ready to shoot each other and the bar patrons clearing to both sides of the room to avoid being shot. Security was not present at the time, and patrons fled in every direction to avoid injury or worse. Pieper cannot think of many worse situations than this at a place where communities across the nation go to relax and enjoy themselves. Since then, this mall has worked unbelievably hard to fix its tarnished reputation. Unfortunately, that soiled reputation remains to this day. Once a mall has the reputation of being the "bad" or other mall in town, it's hard to get customers to continue to shop there as members of the public are scared of violence.

There are numerous gang-related activities such as these that take place daily in our malls nationwide. In 2009, a gang member whom had been arrested on felony charges agreed to speak to gang investigators about his activities for the possibility of a reduced sentence. During this interview, this gang member stated that he often went to the area mall for gang-related activities. One such activity was gang initiations. He would drive aspiring gang members to the mall for a test of bravery and merit in order to be initiated into the gang. In order to join the gang, they would have to find and fight a rival gang member at the mall. Once a rival was located, the aspiring member would confront the rival gang member and a fight would then ensue. If the "probate" failed to fight the rival, he would not be accepted into the gang. During the interview, investigators were also told that this gang member also went to the mall to start fights with rival gang members, as he enjoyed fighting. He would not carry a gun on his person but would keep one in the car in case the need arose. Once he would locate any rival(s), he would challenge them by insulting them and their gang. Fights would then always break out, and he claimed to always be on the winning side. When asked what did this do for him or his gang, he replied that the gang's reputation was further enhanced as was his. Also rival gangs would respect both him and his gang more, respect being equated to fear. In the gang world, one does not have respect without fear. This gang member was never observed by mall security or law enforcement. No reports were ever made and until he told investigators of these actions, they had gone undetected. When asked why he would pick the mall, he stated that he knew it was where people of his age group often went and was the easiest location to find rivals during the daytime hours. The mall had no security in the parking lot areas, so he would often cruise the parking lot looking for cars belonging to rival gang members. Once he found one, he would sit and wait. This information was later passed along to mall staff in order them to be aware of the situations that were occurring. However, no follow-up by mall security or training occurred with this new information. This was a missed opportunity for the mall which later saw more gang-related violence. Violence that might have been prevented had the mall administration taken a serious look at the information it was being given.

Gangs use malls as they use people, with little regard for the outcome of their actions or the problems they create. Often, when a gang's presence at a mall is noticeable to the public, those malls will see declining sales and revenue. As the problem becomes worse either through gang violence, intimidation, or in some cases extortion of the shop owner through "taxes" to be paid to the gang, stores will close up shop and leave. The gang's reputation will often prevent other stores from opening at the same location. This type of situation has occurred at malls in several locations across the United States and continues to this day nationwide.

Mall supervisors and administration often refuse to see the gang problem and as a result, the situation often festers and grows. Situations like this often make one think of the "broken window theory." This theory indicates that maintaining and monitoring urban environments in a well-ordered condition may stop further vandalism and escalation into more serious crime. Likewise, when gangs go unchecked in any mall, often small unchecked issues become larger issues. However, having a well-thought-out and well-executed plan to deal with gangs and gang members can save mall administrators time, resources, and money (especially from potential law suits).

Security personnel are often overworked and ill trained for the gang problem. The turnover rate at some malls is unusually high as well, resulting in any training that the security force receives to be needed over and over again. This is something that due to financial costs and time away from doing actual site protection, many in the mall administration would rather turn a blind eye to.

As a result, training on gangs needs to be done often and on a regular basis. Often, the training that the security team receives does not include how to talk to gang members, what to discuss and what not to discuss, and how to properly document these encounters. Nor does the training include proper "officer safety" which includes showing security personnel how to properly stand when talking with a suspected gang member. Furthermore, the training also lacks what to be cognizant of when having one of these encounters. Details such as what the subject was wearing and his or her tattoos maybe over looked. Another problem is the lack of information about the encounters security has with gang members. This information is rarely passed on to the local Gang Unit or law enforcement. This critical training and information is a must for all mall security to have and should be constantly updated. The benefit to the security teams from this type of additional officer safety training could be tremendous. It builds confidence and morale which pays tenfold when these same personnel are face to face with gang members and gang-type situations. Having well-trained staff with experience and training can save a mall or save a life.

Today, gangs are more violent, more dangerous, and better armed. Mall security is typically seen by the gang as lacking in training and experience. Additionally, due to a typically high turnover rate, good-quality security personnel in this field are hard to find. Without good training and experience in the area of investigation and identification of gangs and gang members, gang problems often go unchecked, unidentified, and can only grow worse.

In March 2008, police did a sweep of the Southdale Mall of America in Bloomington, Minnesota. This sweep was conducted by the Metro Gang Strike Force which was comprised of 13 different law enforcement departments. During this sweep, 30 known gang members were arrested after a gang shooting had occurred at the mall just one month previously. The shooting and gang sweep that resulted from the shooting may have been avoided, had the mall administration implemented a well-thought-out anti-gang policy that included preventive measures, protocols, and procedures for dealing with the gang threat. Had the security personnel had proper anti-gang training (dealing with gangs) prior to the incident, this horrible situation may have been avoided. As is often the case, the gang sweep in this instance is only a short-term solution at best and will only keep the gangs away until the gangs recognize that the law enforcement threat is gone. Maintaining a law enforcement presence, such as the Gang Strike Task Force, is unrealistic and sends the wrong message to the families that go to the mall to have fun and enjoy themselves. When a proper plan is in effect to prevent the gangs from congregating or conducting business to further the criminal enterprise at the mall, no visible law enforcement presence is necessary except the occasional security officer doing his rounds or for the occasional patrol officer making an arrest for the everyday shoplifter.

Training in the areas of gangs and how they affect malls and the surrounding areas is vital in today's world. Often today's training is too short or very narrow, focusing on one specific area and not broad enough to encompass the spectrum of issues that face malls and shopping areas when dealing with gangs and gang members. Trainers often fail to take the time to sit down with the mall security prior to the training to determine what the nature of the problems appears to be. They also fail to take a tour of the mall for which they are providing the training. By looking at the mall patrons and areas of concern, they could provide a more in-depth view to the mall staff on what the problems are presently and how to adequately deal with such problems. Mall administrators often look for the short-term fix by calling local law enforcement to provide short-term, one-hour training. This type of training is often insufficient at best and may be done with several years having gone by since the last training occurred. Mall training in the areas of threats such as gangs and active shooters is vital for all mall personnel. Mall security is too often the only ones that receive the training, but this mistake is starting to be fixed nationwide as well. From administrators to mall custodians, everyone needs to be trained on what to look for in these types of situations and how to identify and solve the gang issue.

Due to the lack of education and training on how to best deal with their gang problems, many malls have elected to merely place signs outside mall entrance doors, indicating the type of clothing and behavior that is acceptable and not acceptable at that location, with the idea that this will curb potential problems and possibly deter thugs and gang members from promoting their bad behavior on those premises. Nothing could be further from the truth, however. These signs are often in small print and go unnoticed by most patrons who don't take the time to read such signs. Most believe the signs do not pertain to them or are in too much of a hurry. As a result, these signs do nothing to curb the unwanted behavior or unwanted persons from entering the mall.

Moreover, threat assessments are rarely done in conjunction with this training. As a result, the security officers receiving the training are not given the whole picture of what the true threats may be. CARVER threat assessments are hardly ever done for malls and are an unused benefit that would go far toward showing the administration and mall staff what the true threats are and how to defend against the threats that these types of assessments will show.

Law enforcement nationwide is starting to see that they alone are not the answer to the gang problem. Gangs are not just a police problem but a community problem. In order for a community to take back any area from gangs, it must be involved. The same goes for malls. Mall personnel must see that the information that they learn and obtain from the encounters and dealings with gang members is vital and should be passed along to other staff and law enforcement alike. Mall personnel should be taught that gangs and gang members will not be tolerated at the mall. There should be a "zero tolerance" for any gang-related activities at the mall and a 100% prosecution of any gang members or gang associates at the mall. Shops that have a no prosecution policy for fear of retaliation or the likes should be told that it is the mall's policy that should crime occur in their store that they will be expected to prosecute and not be allowed to let the gangs know that this mall or any mall will allow their criminal behavior anymore. All too often in many malls across the United States, stores have a zero prosecution policy that promotes criminal behavior. One such retail store is well known worldwide with stores in every state and numerous counties. By allowing the gangs and other criminals alike to have free reign in their stores, this policy does nothing to help the mall or community stop the problems that they are fighting so hard to try and prevent. This store and many others like it are under the false illusion that the money that they lose to theft of product(s) and or damage will be monetarily less than having a zero tolerance policy, training staff to watch for shop lifters, and/or having a well-trained loss prevention staff in place. The money that stores like this lose is tremendous and does nothing to curb any form of criminal behavior. It may even promote it in some cases.

On the brighter side though, malls nationwide are starting to see the issues discussed here and take note. Training of mall staff from the top down is starting to occur on a more regular basis. Gangs that had a foothold in numerous malls are starting to lose their "turf" back to the shop keepers and patrons who love to go to the community's focal points. As time goes on, malls that have the proper training and the right people for the job will prosper no matter where they are located. Gangs cannot get a foothold in malls where they are constantly kept in check and under constant scrutiny. Gang members will often refuse to go to areas where they know that there is a high risk of being observed by security and law enforcement. Gangs under observation by security and law enforcement typically will move on to other locations in order to further their criminal interests. When this occurs, mall shops and stores often see results such as high sales, new shops, and a mall willing to invest new money into its property and people.

Nation of Islam

Most gangs today band together to make money by various criminal enterprises. As we have seen recently in Chicago, gangs have banded together to provide weapons and other resources such as snipers to execute unsuspecting law enforcement officers responding to calls for service. A new trend that is positive on face value are gangs banding together for truces and positive change in the community. According to an article published in *Inspire* on August 9, 2016 by Tony Muhammad entitled "L. A. Street Organizations Move Forward in Efforts for Peace by Charlene Muhammad." Nation of Islam Western Region Student Minister asked how many had lost a loved one due to gang violence at a meeting in July 2016. Days later various organizations held their first follow-up meeting after the Honorable Minister Louis Farrakhan put out an historic call through student Min. Muhammad for the so-called gangs to unite and stop the violence. The house was packed for the session hosted by student Min. Muhammad. It was heavily attended by gang intervention specialists, community activists, leaders, and concerned citizens looking for an end to violence and real change in their communities. "I'm honored beyond words to see friends of mine, who I know, are front line soldiers, because we've got a deep, deep problem in our community, and it runs so deep, that it takes us back hundreds of years," student Min. Muhammad said. On a large poster board depicting the 1995 Million Man March Pledge, members of the street organizations signed the "Bloods & Crips 2016 Peace Treaty" on July 17th Cease Fire Agreement.

> We're dealing with the residual effects of a destroyed people … and we, both Black and Brown and Red have been beat down so far, that we have somewhat taken on the mind of those who dominated us, and now we are on remote control doing it to ourselves.
>
> Min. Muhammad

The message of peace, love, and respect was conveyed by speaker after speaker, who spoke with a sense of urgency to the audience during the initial July 17th meeting. The article goes on to say Min. Muhammad said he called the Bloods and Crips on behalf of the Honorable Minister Louis Farrakhan. "The plan is to coordinate the best practices from everyone who has already been putting in work to solve the problem of violence in South Central," student Min. Muhammad said. He urged everyone to work together in their lane for the overall goal. "Yes! Police have got to back up off of us, but, at the same time … ain't no cameras around … when we're looking at a bloody body," he stated. Indigenous community activists and organizers, including Alex Sanchez of the gang intervention effort Homies Unidos, have consistently worked in the streets helping the community. The room was filled with hope and sparks of creativity as many excitedly discussed ways to improve not just the streets, but their homes, families, and the well-being of individuals. Some ideas included community policing and education, recycling black dollars, economic development, creating re-entry programs, developing job, education, and financial resource hubs, community gardening and urban farming, and launching youth programs. "Be patient with each other, and shun money as a motive," Min. Muhammad encouraged. "If that's your motive, the government will sucker you into the money, and then control you, and give you just enough to fail," he said. "Credit for the good works they were planning goes solely to God and the purpose is to unite, not create a new organization." The 2016 gang truce came in the midst of his work to galvanize peace throughout the streets of Los Angeles, including monthly Southern California Peace Rides. The Peace Rides, which include groups and clubs who ride motorcycles, low riders, mini bikes, and drive Corvettes, are coordinated in conjunction with the Southern California Cease Fire Committee and a host of organizations, activists, and artists and culminates in a park rally for peace called UPFest.

This is an uplifting article in *Inspire* regarding gang truces but was met with some skepticism by all three authors. How do you maintain these truces when the gang's criminal enterprises to make money will be disrupted at their own hands? It just doesn't seem viable nor sustainable given the propensity for gang members to get rich quick by any means possible. You also have to look at the possible true root cause. If rival gangs keep banding together to target law enforcement similar to the snipers in Chicago, you can foresee that the Fraternal Order of Police organizations may prompt a walk out of police officers nationwide. The public at large would be in jeopardy and mass chaos which would prompt martial law to be implemented. Collectively, we hope the message in the *Inspire* article is genuine. Although, it is possible that fear of the big picture for minorities is more representative of reality. Martial law impeding their freedom 24/7 by the federal government is likely the motivator.

6   First Contact

Hugo and Carlos

Up to this point Pieper's interactions with Carlos had been mostly non-eventful. Previously Pieper had been dispatched to a report of a domestic disturbance where it was alleged that Carlos had kneed his sister in the crotch and took off on foot. However, that was about all the interaction with this gang member that Pieper had been present for. The subject that he was talking with was wearing a blue and white Peyton Manning jersey with black Dickie pants, white Nike Cortez sneakers with blue laces, and a blue Sur 13 bandanna hanging out of his back right pocket. Pieper had asked the subject his name and he stated with confidence, Hugo Duges. Pieper asked Hugo how old he was and Hugo stated that he was "thirteen plus one." This struck Pieper as odd as he had never been very good at math, but he did realize that Hugo was 14 years old. Pieper hadn't even asked Hugo if he was also a member of Sur 13. He hadn't needed to as Hugo had thrown it out there in his own way for everyone to know. Hugo was so proud of his gang membership and so disgusted with his rivals Norte 14, that he wouldn't even say the word "fourteen." This set the tone for the relationship that Pieper was able to have for the following years with Hugo. By Hugo saying that one phrase "thirteen plus one" he told Pieper exactly what his mindset was and just how loyal to the gang Hugo was and would be in the coming years (Figure 6.1).

Up until this point Pieper had only heard of Hugo, this was in part because Hugo was vastly turning into a habitual runaway whose name was being read off in squad meetings on a weekly basis, if not daily basis, for patrolmen to look out for. Pieper asked Hugo what his street name was and he replied "Hugo." Pieper had dispatch run Hugo and Carlos for warrants and Hugo was reported as a runaway. As Pieper was waiting, dispatch to tell him the status of Hugo and Carlos, he asked them what they were doing walking through rival gang turf at 1:30 in the morning. Hugo and Carlos looked at each other as if they didn't know what to say. Pieper asked them if they did in fact know that they were walking through rival territory and they replied "yes." A search of Hugo and Carlos revealed that they had no weapons or drugs. Pieper told them that it was pretty stupid to be walking through East Side Crip turf. East Side Crips and the Brown Pride Locos (a gang aligned with the East Side Crips) were known for their violent tendencies that usually ended in gun fire.

Figure 6.1 Hugo with Detective Pieper.

Seeing that Hugo was reported as a runaway and Carlos was a juvenile out at 1:30 in the morning walking through rival turf, Pieper took them home. Carlos lived at 2809 9th Ave E so Pieper took him home first. After knocking on the door several times his mother answered and naturally looked as if she had just been woken up. Carlos's mother didn't seem too bothered that the police were bringing her son home in the wee hours of the morning, after catching him in rival gang territory. Carlos's mother let him in the house and quickly shut the door in Pieper's face. Pieper then took Hugo home, he lived nearby. Pieper knocked on the door and Hugo's mother, opened up the door almost immediately. She then grabbed Hugo and pulled him inside asking him where he had been and who he was with. Hugo didn't have much to say as he looked down to the ground. He couldn't even look his mother in the eye. At this time Pieper knew that Hugo's mother loved him very much and was very worried about him. Pieper could also tell that Hugo felt bad about what he was putting his mother through. Hugo's mother was clearly worried and asked Pieper all the questions that a "normal" concerned mother would. "Where was my son?" "Is he in trouble?" "What can I do to help the situation?" and so on. From that moment on Pieper knew that this would not be the last time that he was going to deal with Hugo or Carlos but there was something about Hugo that told Pieper that he was going to be a handful.

This first encounter with both parents was important. While both encounters were brief during this incident, both Plonczynski and Pieper would later have numerous interactions with both. Both parents were total opposites of one another as the detectives would find out over the coming years. Hugo's mother was caring to her son and the law enforcement that routinely came to her door. She would invite the officers in, offer them food or coffee, and give them permission to search the home every time they came over. She had nothing to hide and if her family was breaking the law, she wanted nothing to do with it. She was the type of parent that we all would be proud of. She was regularly in poor health, however. When Plonczynski, AKA Ski, would go to Hugo's home looking for him, the first thing she would do is hug him and ask why he didn't have a wife yet. She was caring and an amazing person to be around. She had little money for the family but as the only parent in the house, she worked as hard as she could and often gave everything she could to her family.

Carlos's mother, however, was not the same. She often would do what she could to protect her children from the law. She appeared to play favorites among her own kids as well as giving everything she could to Carlos, often at the expense of the other children. All three of her kids would go on and grow up to be gang members. She was what many people think of as a parent to a gang member.

Prior to this incident Hugo had been running the streets "putting in work" for the gang. He was running away from home, fighting at school, using marijuana and almost every time he was out, he was with Carlos. In one brazen incident in 2005, Hugo and Carlos were riding their bikes to the house of a fellow gang member at about 2:30 in the afternoon. While riding their bikes Hugo reached into his pocket, pulled out a gun, and began to rip several shots off into the air. Hugo didn't realize as he did this that he rode right by a marked sheriff's vehicle. Hugo and Carlos continued to ride their bikes and before the deputy could catch up to them Hugo was able to ditch the gun but not the 93 rounds he had in his pocket. Over the years Hugo became notorious for this kind of activity.

On November 28, 2006 at about 5:36 pm, Hugo was observed driving a maroon Cadillac with a white canvas top and a New Mexico license plate. This vehicle was known to belong to the leader of Sur 13, 17th St clique. This vehicle was well known on the streets from Brownsville to Bradenton, Wimouma to Tampa. A vigilant patrolman observed Hugo driving the vehicle in the 1200 block of 12th St W. It was well known to area law enforcement that Hugo did not possess a valid driver's license. Come to think of it, after all of these years Hugo never did get his license. This patrolman noticed that there were several subjects in the vehicle and conducted a traffic stop. Lo and behold it was a who's who of Sur 13 gang members inside the vehicle and two fully loaded guns. Hugo was arrested for driving without a valid driver's license. Other subjects in the vehicle included:

1   Eduardo - Sur 13, 17th St clique (arrested for CCF)
2   Noel - Sur 13, 17th St clique (arrested for CCF)
3   Eduardo's father
4   Carlos - Sur 13 17th St clique
5   Gilberto - leader of Sur 13 17th St clique

One can only imagine what they were getting ready to do that night or had done earlier. There were no reported drive-by shootings that night, although many shootings where rival gang members and families were the victims went unreported.

On January 6, 2007, Pieper was working in an undercover capacity as a "John" in an attempt to pick up shall we say, ladies of the evening. For most law enforcement officers this is a great time, it's just about as low key and nonviolent of an operation as there can be. It's the ultimate game of chess and you're battling wits with some very street-savvy ladies. Trick one, no pun intended, is that you have to get them in your car. Then you have to make a deal for a sexual act. Needless to say, it's not always as easy as it looks. Throughout the course of the night Pieper was only able to land one or two arrests. He had gotten two calls from Ski telling him that they had a drive-by shooting in Oneco at a Quinceañera but nobody was injured. This type of incident in that part of town was not uncommon. Pieper told him that he was a bit tied up but that if he needed any assistance he would take off his "jorts"—jean shorts, wife beater, and cowboy hat and change over and help Ski out.

About thirty minutes later dispatch sent patrol units to an armed robbery call. The dispatcher advised that the victim was shot, possibly in the head. The unit Pieper was working with was only a couple of blocks away so immediately they responded. Upon arrival Pieper observed a Hispanic male laying on the ground with a large amount of blood coming out of his head. The victim had been on the wrong end of an armed robbery when he and his friend tried to fight back. The coward shot him in the head and his friend in the buttocks. As Pieper was assisting patrol, Ski called again. Thinking that Ski needed assistance Pieper answered and asked him, "What's up?" Pieper never forgot the tone of his voice when he said, "Dude, I know what you're dealing with over there in the city as I heard it over the radio but we just had another drive-by, this time it was in Palmetto." The first shooting had only occurred about 1 ½ hours earlier so this was clearly in retaliation for the Quinceañera shooting. What no one knew was if the armed robbery was related to any of this as well.

Pieper hightailed it back to the office and changed clothes as it was clear that he was done picking up prostitutes for the evening. Pieper got in his car and drove back to the robbery scene. There wasn't much for him to do as he doesn't speak Spanish and the suspects were unknown. He decided to go to the "tree."

The "tree" is located deep in gang territory in the city limits. Just as the name indicates, there is a giant tree growing there. What makes this tree stand out is that it is growing in the middle of the road. There's no median in the street, just this big tree splitting the road. When the city originally put the road there, they clearly had gotten lazy and rather than cut the tree down, they just paved around it. Next to the "tree" lived Bobby Black. Bobby was a high-ranking member of Sur 13's Terras Blancos Locos clique. Pieper knew this area to be popular for Sur 13 gang members to hang out at because it was off of the beaten path and hard to sneak up on. Once Pieper pulled up he noticed three or four female Sur 13 gang members hanging out. Over the years he had developed a decent rapport with some of them and we began to talk. Pieper asked where all the guys were and they said that they went to Ybor City to party. Let's stop and discuss this fact gentle reader. First of all, how do you know when a gang member is lying? Simple, their lips are moving. Gang members are typically poor. When they have money, it gets spent very fast. It's not like they have high paying jobs or income that they can spend frivolously on. It was really easy for Pieper to know that this was a total lie and he continued to talk to them as if he hadn't heard of the earlier shootings.

While they were talking he noticed a newer black pickup truck pull up to Bobby Black's house. The vehicle was pointed right at Pieper's police vehicle in the driveway. Pieper was unable to see who was in it, but knew the truck wasn't there to make a Tupperware sale. Upon seeing Pieper, the vehicle quickly backed out of the resident's driveway. Pieper knew talking to the girls was a dead end and jumped into his car and followed the pickup. As he tailed them, he looked for a traffic infraction that would give him a legal reason for the stop. Pieper could have just stopped them if there was reason to believe they were involved in any crime. At this point though, there was no such evidence of such and as this was the case he continued to watch and wait for an infraction to occur. Any good beat cop will tell you that gang members often are bad drivers. They don't believe that the laws apply to them and as such, drive the way they want to drive. However, this wasn't the case here. This pickup stopped properly for every posted stop sign, maintained a single lane, and was not playing their music. Thinking back, they must have been so proud of themselves for acting like such fine upstanding citizens however; they forgot just one detail. The state of Florida like many other states has a strict window tint law. In this case, the tint on the windows appeared to be below the legal limit. Even though it was dark out it's still a traffic violation and probable cause for a stop. Pieper initiated a traffic stop and called out his location to dispatch and called for backup units as he didn't have any clue who was in the vehicle, and it had just pulled into and then left a known gang house. Pieper knew whoever it was had to be gang related one way or another. As he was approaching the driver, Pieper noticed what appeared to be several very fresh bullet holes in the vehicle. They were so fresh that the paint around them was still peeling off and flapping in the wind. Pieper cautiously made contact with the driver, Cris Vallez, who was a member of the West Side Locos (a local gang who were at the time aligned with Sur 13). Pieper then noticed Hugo, Carlos, and Gilberto in the vehicle. Seeing four gang members in one vehicle, what appear to be fresh bullet holes in the side of the pickup, and having known about two shootings just previous to this stop, Pieper thought he had won the jackpot. Back up units arrived and quickly took up a flanking position on the other side of the vehicle to see inside and watch the subjects. As the backup officers peered into the passenger side window, one of the officers advised Pieper that he saw a semiautomatic firearm next to Carlos's foot in the front passenger seat of the vehicle. This is another red flag now. Guns drawn, Pieper and his backup units slowly and carefully had everybody exit the vehicle. Once outside of the truck, officers placed the occupants of the truck in handcuffs. What came next was no shocker, Carlos as it turned out actually had an outstanding warrant so he was going to be arrested no matter what. The firearm was quickly photographed where it was located, then carefully checked to be cleared and as it turned out, had no rounds in it. Let's take a minute here to talk about this. A firearm has many uses to a gang member. It serves as a deterrent when flashed to rivals, it serves as protection when being shot at by rivals or law enforcement, and it serves as a tool for vengeance when shooting at rivals when the gang members do drive-bys. There are several other uses but you get the point. That being said, currently this firearm was being used as a paperweight. That is to say, that everyone would agree that a gun without ammunition is for the most part useless. Gang members are not typically in the habit of carrying unloaded guns. In fact, most common sense law enforcement officers would venture to say gang members are very street savvy and as such would usually make sure that their gun or guns are fully loaded. As such, the question that begs to be asked is this: was the gun just used or was it intentionally carried without ammo for whatever reason?

Pieper quickly got on the phone and called Ski. Ski answered on the first ring and Pieper notified him of who had been stopped and the circumstances surrounding the traffic stop. Ski was ecstatic and quickly explained that he believed that the subjects that Pieper had stopped were the suspects in the Palmetto shooting and the vehicle they were in also matched the description that the witnesses of the shooting had given deputies. Ski and the rest of the Sheriff's Office Gang Unit then quickly responded to the traffic stops location. Together both agencies began trying to put together the case. Working quickly now that there was more than enough manpower on the scene, Ski had patrol deputies from the Sheriff's Office bring the victim from the Palmetto shooting to their location to do a "show up."

A show up is when the victim of a crime is able to view a possible suspect to a crime that had just occurred. There are lots of legal guidelines that go along with doing a show up, but in this case everything was righteous and the victim of the shooting, without hesitation, picked out Gilberto, Carlos, and Hugo as being present for the shooting. The victim stated that they were walking behind the pickup truck, as Hugo without provocation or reason just started shooting at them. The victims weren't able to identify Cris Vallez. Most likely, he was the driver of the truck and they just weren't able to see him from where they were or while they were running for their lives from flying bullets. As the show up was being conducted Hugo could be seen standing out in front of the Sheriff's Office patrol vehicle. He was standing there just waiting to be viewed by the victims of the shooting to see if he was identified as the shooter or having been present.

As he stood there he was flashing his gang hand signs in plain view of everyone present who could see him. Not only did his fellow gang members see this, but law enforcement and several shooting witnesses observed him as well. He did this with his hands behind his back but had turned around to show everyone what he was doing. This was a bold move. This action showed the other gang members he was "down" for the gang. It showed law enforcement that he was going to remain a hardcore member of the gang, and lastly it showed the witnesses something they wouldn't forget. He was a gang member (Figure 6.2).

Gilberto, Carlos, and Hugo were all arrested and taken to Bradenton Police Department's main station for interviewing and processing. All that he would say is that they were the ones that were shot at and he would answer the required questions for the paperwork. Ski and Pieper then got ready to talk to Hugo. Up to this point and time Pieper had read Hugo his rights about 45 times prior to this incident. He had never agreed to talk to any law enforcement to our knowledge. This time was no different. Before anyone had wasted any time with Hugo, Pieper asked him if he was willing to talk to them, if they read him his rights. He looked at Pieper and asked him to repeat himself. There was no doubt that everyone knew he had heard what Pieper had asked him, but it was like it was some kind of game to him to see if he could get Pieper to repeat himself. Naturally, Pieper did and Hugo still looked at him. Pieper then said, "Look Hugo, I know you understand me, I'm not speaking a foreign language here, if we read you your rights are

Figure 6.2 Hugo (Left), El Jefe (Middle), and Manny (Right).

you going to talk to us?" Hugo looked at him with a smug look on his face and said, "you know I'm not going to talk, Pieper." Carlos was brought in next and the two gang detectives got ready to interview Carlos. Ski and Pieper read him his rights and he agreed to talk to them. They interviewed him for the better part of two hours. He was on the fence of telling the seasoned investigators what really happened but in the end he gave them nothing. Let's call it what it is, these subjects knew that if they kept their mouth shut they would most likely get their charges dropped. Gilberto was not arrested that night as there had been no probable cause for him. Carlos went on his warrant and Hugo went on the shooting charge. In the end all the charges were dropped and the community continued to be plagued by further gang violence (Figures 6.3 and 6.4).

Figure 6.3 Gun, Body Armor, and Sur 13 Bandanna Located on Traffic Stop with Carlos and Sur 13 Gang Members.

Figure 6.4 Hugo and Another Sur 13 Gang Member "Posting Up" in Front of Pieper's Car During a Traffic Stop.

Javier

The first time Javier had an encounter with law enforcement was in 2003, when he was told in school that his gang "sucked" by another child. Javier responded to this insult against his gang and his reputation with a back slap across the other child's face. The child was knocked down by the blow. Law enforcement responded and Javier was charged with Battery, however the state attorney's office declined to file the charge and Javier never saw any repercussions for the action. Javier was only 11 years old. The product of a household where the father was always off drinking elsewhere or cheating and a mother who worked full time and then some to support four children. No one knew it yet, but here was a monster in the making.

It wasn't three months later when Javier and his brother were observed by school staff spray painting "Southside 13" on the outside of their elementary school wall. They were marking their turf and letting everyone know that their gang was the biggest and the baddest. Once again the law was called. Once again charges were filed, and once again the state attorney's office declined to file charges. One month later while in school, Javier would be ordered by his brother to punch a child that had disrespected Sur 13. Javier had hit the child so hard that the child had to go home and possibly to the hospital. Charges were pressed, and as had happened before, the system dropped the ball. Three encounters with the law, three times there was no justice, no repercussions, and no reason to stop his behavior.

Only months later, Bradenton Police Department was called to Javier's home. His mother had called 911 after Javier and his brother had gotten in to a verbal argument with their mother. She had tried to discipline Javier. Javier was past the point of allowing anyone to discipline him though. He attacked his mother and grabbed her by the neck to prevent her from striking him. Javier took a ride to the Juvenile Booking Facility and served 21 days. He was later given probation by the court. However, as Javier's mother, the court, law enforcement, and the community in which Javier lived were destined to learn, probation was neither a deterrent nor effective in trying to stop this growing menace (Figure 6.5).

In the following weeks, Bradenton Police were called to Javier's home again. A family member had found a shotgun in Javier's bedroom. While on scene and in a parent's presence, the patrolman read Javier his Miranda warning. Javier was honest and he told both the officer and his mom the truth. There are members of the rival Brown Pride Locos street gang that would shoot him if possible and he needed this shotgun for protection against them. He bought the gun in the worst part of town for $140.00. Javier was then arrested for a minor being in possession of a loaded firearm. After this arrest, he was released and he purchased another shotgun. It was shortly after this occurred that Plonczynski met Javier.

The first time Plonczynski met Javier was in 2006. It was a bright sunny day around 10 am. Talk about amazing weather. It was the kind of day that demanded beach time, not office time. The problem was that beach time didn't pay as well. Plonczynski had been in the office working alone for a couple days. His partner

Figure 6.5 Javier after Being Stopped During a Gang Violation Beating.

had taken time off and he was forced to do the work of two people for the time being. It was around midmorning when he got a call from the dispatcher to go to a shared law enforcement channel on my portable radio to talk to officers in the Bradenton Police Department. The city of Bradenton was located in the county that he worked. He was a bit curious as he went to my portable radio because he had no idea why city cops would want a Sheriff's Deputy. As he got on the radio, he identified himself and asked what they needed. He was told that four Bradenton Officers had been dispatched to a house in reference to a runaway. The only issue was that when they got there, none of the kids would talk to the officers. They suspected that the four were gang members and were hoping that he would be able to identify them as they were all under arrest now. He explained that he would respond and asked where the call was. This call was pretty odd to him as Bradenton's Police Department had a Gang Unit and moreover, a Gang Unit that would be able to identify their own gang members much better than he could have. He wasn't exactly sure why they weren't calling their own people but he responded all the same. When he arrived on scene, he first spoke to the officers.

Originally, when he got there, things were a little tense. Upon getting out of the car, he immediately noticed that these officers seemed very frustrated and irritated. As he spoke to one of Bradenton's Uniform Patrol Officers, he was informed that one of the officers had been in the house earlier when an incident occurred. While his partner had been outside dealing with the three others he had been speaking to the sole male of the group, Javier. Javier, not happy about the fact that the police were in his room, in his house, or on his property had decided to spice things up a little and while being questioned by the patrolman, he had lunged for a nearby shotgun. Mind you, Javier was only 14 years old at this point. There had been a struggle and even though Javier was 14 years old he wasn't all that small. He was about 5 feet and 5 inches tall. Genetics had not been unkind and he had a decent amount of muscle and girth to him even at this young of an age. Javier may have had the element of surprise but the officer was quicker, bigger, and stronger and was able to wrestle the 12-gauge shotgun away from Javier and then get back up and get Javier handcuffed and arrested.

These officers couldn't believe that these fearless four children were giving them so much hassle. It wasn't even four teenagers, as one of them was an 11-year-old girl.

While speaking to the patrolmen, Plonczynski was told that they initially had gotten a call about a runaway or runaways being present. Not the type of call where a gun is usually in play. As Plonczynski later found out, two of the four were runaways including the 11-year-old girl (whom we'll call Sadie). When Bradenton Police Department had arrived, all four kids refused to speak to the officers or give them any information including their names. One of the officers had told me that all were from the criminal street gang Sur 13. Plonczynski went from juvenile to juvenile. All were in handcuffs. Two were sitting in the back seats of marked cars and the others were sitting apart from each other smiling as big as they could grin. They loved messing with Bradenton police officers. It was funny. The county deputies never seemed to get the hassle that the city officers did. No one ever knew why. An oddity that still occurs to this day I think.

As he went from juvenile to juvenile, he didn't recognize any of them at first. Although, all would play large roles in the criminal street gang Sur 13 as they got older, and shape the city and county's gang world in pretty big ways.

As Plonczynski went to the first two juveniles in an attempt to identify them, he started to worry. He had no idea as to who these kids were. Until this moment, Plonczynski had usually dealt with gang members that had been a little older. These kids were young, which was half the issue. They had no fear of the repercussions of their actions and they were pretty smug about it. Plonczynski thought he wasn't going to be much help until he saw that last one of the four. She was the one that saved his reputation that day. She was hard to miss. She was fifteen but stood taller than him. Mind you he isn't a tall guy but female early teenagers aren't standing taller than him for the most part. He had met her once before, after she was arrested for a home invasion robbery. Yes, you read that right. This 15-year-old girl had already been arrested for a 1st degree felony and was still out on the street.

On the one incident that Plonczynski had the pleasure of meeting her, she had just been arrested. She had gone into a home with three other gang members that night. The two girls had been decoys on that occasion. They had gone to a mobile home where they had learned drugs were being sold out of. Where there are drugs, there usually is money and guns as well. They had gone to a gang house earlier that night and planned out the "lick" (slang for the crime). After all had been planned out, she and another girl had gone to the front door and knocked on it. Being teenage girls, the occupants had opened the door and not expected anything. What they didn't know was that two Sur 13 gang members had accompanied the females and were in the bushes nearby with guns. When the door was opened, the males jumped out and all four rushed in. We won't get in to details about this incident other than to say that she was caught and Plonczynski had interviewed her after the fact. However, this is a story for another time.

Needless to say that on this date, Plonczynski remembered her. As he spoke to her he asked her if she remembered him. She said that she had never met him before. He called her bluff and explained how they had previously met. She lost her smugness at this point and turned 180 degrees in her attitude. She had been nice, quiet, and peaceful until this point. Now that he knew who she was and her game was up, she started spitting vulgar statements and calling him every name in the book. Plonczynski used a zinger on her and asked her if she kissed her mother with that mouth. She continued making insults about him and the other officers there. That was one down. Plonczynski then went back to Javier. He stood in handcuffs on the sidewalk with a Bradenton officer behind him. Plonczynski stated who he was and explained that he was with the Sheriff's Office Gang Unit. Javier was cool as a mountain stream. Javier may have enjoyed the fact that a Gang Unit detective had been present and that he was getting all this attention now. In truth, he had Plonczynski's full attention already as not too many 14-year-old boys try to pull guns on cops. At least not any Plonczynski had met at that point. Javier told Plonczynski that his street name is "Crazy Loco." He had given him his real name but it wasn't until later that Plonczynski learned his real street moniker. As he told Plonczynski his real name, the officer behind him stood there in disbelief. He had been hounding Javier for some time trying to get just basic information from him, like his name. However, Javier had kept his mouth shut. As a cop, we have to give props where they are due here. Javier pulled a gun on a fellow law enforcement brother. This is a big problem. However, rather than trying to teach this 14-year-old a lesson, the officer's had shown true professionalism and kept their collective cool. They were pissed off, to put it mildly and maybe said a few things (before Plonczynski got there) to Javier. This can be said though: Javier did not have a hand laid on him after the gun struggle was over. These guys were true blue and kept their cool after the fact. Usually when you play well with the bad guys, there can be a bit of mutual respect. Javier had none for Bradenton's Police

Department. He was just fine talking to Plonczynski though. A point that Plonczynski exploited too. Plonczynski asked him if he was in a gang and he stated he was a person of rank in the 17th Street clique of Sur 13. Javier was smug and friendly. He had a bit of charm to him.

Plonczynski then went back to the house to speak to the 11-year-old female that had been in handcuffs sitting on the porch steps with a big smile on her face. She seemed to be enjoying the situation which was really disturbing to him. Juveniles this young, acting in this manner, are a big red flag to anyone with half a brain cell in their head. All these kids were acting this way too. It didn't occur to anyone yet, but these kids were already way off on the "moral compass." Plonczynski asked her what her name was and she gave it to him truthfully and without a second thought. Once again, the patrolman who stood next to Plonczynski thought he was some magician getting this information as these kids refused to give word one to the Bradenton officers. The patrolman ran her information and found that additionally, this one was indeed listed as a runaway. No worries here as she had been arrested by Bradenton anyway.

Plonczynski went into the house with one of the Bradenton patrolmen. Inside, Javier's mom was there. She had been the one that had called 911 about the two runaways earlier and had let the officer in the house to speak to Javier. For whatever reason they never had asked mom what the kids names were though, or didn't have the chance to do so. She was cooperative when Plonczynski spoke to her. This would later change as the years went by. She spoke broken English and no one there spoke Spanish but her and the kids. She handed Plonczynski a bunch of papers from Javier's bedroom that she had found. Many years later, these same papers would come back to haunt Javier in a trial, worse than he could have ever imagined or feared. Among these papers were photos of gang members. Pages where Lil Squid declared her undying love for the leader of Sur 13 along with pictures of her throwing up gang hand signs. There were pictures of numerous other girls who were also in the gang. Later, investigators found one piece of paper, however that was better than any photo. Along with everything else was a single piece of paper with a "Roll Call." At the time, gang investigators in the area and patrolman alike knew that some of the Sur 13 clique's members reported to one leader, but this roll call of 56 names spelled it out clearly. All of Sur 13 cliques reported to the leader of the group and that leader reported to "Zeus." This roll call paper showed that Sur 13 had structure. Additionally, this paper gave us 56 names of Sur 13 gang members that confirmed that these people were indeed in the gang. Many names were known on the list, several were not at the time but would later come to be known as Pieper and Plonczynski's careers went on.

Bradenton P.D. started to wrap things up at the house. Plonczynski took the papers Javier's mom had given him and got in the car. All four juveniles had been arrested. Javier was the only one facing anything serious. As I drove to the Juvenile Booking Facility, Plonczynski called Pieper up to let him know what went down. Pieper was pretty livid that his own people had called another Gang Unit out outside of their own agencies to the scene rather than him and his Gang Unit.

He should've been called as it was his jurisdiction but for whatever reason, no one ever called him. Plonczynski went to the Juvenile Booking Facility. There I spoke to Sadie, Javier, Javier's sister Dora, and Chela.

Plonczynski didn't question them about what had happened at the house. In truth that wasn't why he was called to the scene and he was never asked to speak to the kids about what happened. Rather, he spoke to all of them individually and then later all together about being in the gang. Gang members love the attention. It plays to their ego and a bit to their street cred. Not so much the part talking to the cops, that would hurt their street cred, but the part where the cops question them for hours and don't get anything that can be used against them about the crime. Javier was in rare form this day. He was very talkative and spoke at length about being in the gang and even posed for numerous photos while throwing up gang hand signs. He then explained what the hand signs meant and how they were used. In retrospect, the only thing that could have been better is if there was video that day. Unfortunately, that wasn't possible then and would even be a bit hard in today's world to get.

After Plonczynski spoke to Javier, he spoke to the three girls each by themselves. Most male investigators would have cringed at the idea of being alone in a room with a teenage girl. The door to the interview room had a very large window though and the intake deputy could both see and partially hear them.

All three girls also posed and allowed Plonczynski to take pictures of them while throwing up gang hand signs. Each explained that they were all members of the criminal street gang Sur 13 and all were very proud to be members of the 17th Street clique.

At the time, Plonczynski didn't know it but he was talking to four gang members that would have very active criminal careers. Four gang members that would shape both Pieper's and Plonczynski's career in very direct ways. Javier would go on to be a high-ranking leader in his clique. His sister, who was also present that day, would be a leader as well, although much later after Javier was gone. The other two would not take on as important roles in the gang but would both become hardcore gang members that would obtain a lot of respect out on the street and cause the community in which they lived heartache and headaches. Sadie would later have the shortest time on the street. Only 2 years or so later, after being listed as a runaway numerous times and having been arrested countless other times, Sadie got into a physical confrontation with a patrolman. During the arrest, she bit the patrolman, and then attempted to pull his gun out of the holster and use it on him. Needless to say, this did not go well for her. Neither Pieper nor Plonczynski were involved in that trial, but Plonczynski was involved in the sentencing. Her attorney was a public defender. One Plonczynski and Pieper later learned to have a good deal of respect for. She did a great job of trying to discredit Plonczynski while he was on the stand, and to her defense, she did everything she could to try and prove that her client was not a gang member. However, in the end, Plonczynski was recognized as a "gang expert" by the court and thusly, the report, pictures, and subsequent interview from that one day was allowed to be brought in and discussed. While on the stand Plonczynski discussed what he had seen that day and showed the pictures of her throwing up the gang hand signs. In the end, the judge stated that she was "a gang member" in open court, despite what the defense claimed and as such sentenced her accordingly. No one has seen Sadie since and it may be several more years from the time of this writing before anyone not in a correctional setting does.

This was the first time Plonczynski met Javier, but as time went on, it would be far from the last and years from that day, Javier would commit a crime so profound that it would shape and change the community and both Pieper's and Plonczynski's careers.

Sniper

Back in 2004 and 2005 the criminal street gang Sur 13 was growing in membership to numbers that were hard to fathom. At that time in both Pieper and Plonczynski's jurisdictions the gang was amassing new members daily. Crime was rising due to the increasing numbers in not only the street gang but other street gangs as well. Fights between the gangs were common occurrences in the low-income housing areas and were often unreported. Drive-by shootings were also increasing as were other forms of violent crime. Plonczynski had conducted an investigation into one of these drive-bys, where a rival gang member had actually agreed to press charges which back then was just as rare as it is today. In today's world the public believes that law enforcement can solve most crimes without the communities help which everybody knows is nothing but a farce, a falsehood. Since the majority of gang-related crimes are committed on rival gang members, having witnesses to come forward to talk to the police or investigators is a very difficult thing to see and an even more difficult to have go through the entire justice system from beginning to end. In many gang-related cases, the victim may give a truthful statement early on in the case, but will change their story as time goes on. After the arrest is made, witnesses whether they're gang members or not often lose their willingness to cooperate or become scared and fear retribution. In this case the gang leader for the largest gang in the area had conducted a drive-by shooting with two other members of his gang. Spider was well known as the "realist" and most respected member of the criminal street gang Sur 13. Of all the separate cliques, all of whom had different leadership, they all reported to one person, and that was Spider. Prior to Spider becoming leader to all of the cliques, Sur 13 had no separate cliques. It was just one large gang. However, it's members began having issues that were not centralized to the gang itself and the separate cliques splintered off, forming their own hierarchies and leaderships. No one really knows how Spider came into power, but somehow at this point all cliques reported to him.

All gang members are judged based on their street credibility or street cred, as it's also known and Spider was no different. Spider was a fighter, and he was just as violent as the next. What most didn't know about him was that he also had a terminal form of cancer, and was living on borrowed time. In this case he and two other gang members had done a drive-by on a rival Norte 14 gang member's house. Plonczynski had done his homework and investigated as much as possible in the case, and finally was able to obtain probable cause and an arrest warrant for Spider. It was only a short time later that Plonczynski was driving through one of the worst crime-ridden parts of his jurisdiction when he observed an SUV that passed him with all of the windows down. In the back seat, behind the driver, and as plain as day, there was Spider. Plonczynski got behind the vehicle to conduct a traffic stop. Given who was known to be in the vehicle, Plonczynski quickly called for assisting units to back him up. A good friend of Plonczynski's, who is a K-9 handler, and also in the area quickly attached to the call and sped towards the direction that the vehicles were traveling. Another zone unit also attached to the call. As the K-9 handler caught up to Plonczynski he fell in behind him. Knowing additional help was already on the way, a felony traffic stop was conducted. The suspect vehicle came to a stop and Spider was ordered out of the car over the PA system. He opened up the door, and just stood there yelling on his cell phone. As he did so a second marked unit arrived and took a position almost 90° off from where Plonczynski and the K-9 officer were positioned. The K-9 handler had the dog out of the car and continued to give verbal direction. Plonczynski however had his gun pointed directly at the car as did the other backup patrol unit. Spider acted as if they weren't even there and continued to yell into his phone. After a full minute of being ordered to the ground and to drop the phone, Plonczynski was told that the dog could not be released as there was no weapon seen or implied. It was an impasse. The two other gang members that were in the vehicle were high-ranking members of the Island Bound Sureno clique.

As such, both were very violent well-known criminals. Please change to "This was before the days of Plonczynski's agency issuing tasers and patrol cars carrying less than lethal rounds that could have been used for officer safety in this type of situation so it was a bit of a catch-22. Spider continued to yell that officers stopped him unjustly, that he was being harassed. During the yelling tirade, it was obvious that he was talking to someone specific. He made it clear exactly where he was, apparently calling for assistance. In today's law enforcement this is an extremely dangerous situation whereas a person such as a criminal street gang member could be calling in numerous reinforcements. Plonczynski holstered his gun, looked the K-9 handler, and stated, "I got this." He then quickly walked up to where Spider was, and as he came within arm's reach, he went to grab Spider's right arm, and take him into custody. Spider dropped his phone and threw one hell of a fast sucker punch. The punch landed square in the face of Plonczynski and the fight was on. Plonczynski knew that this had to be quick and this had to be fast as the other occupants of the vehicle were no doubt going to get out and start to fight as well. A fight ensued but was over almost as quickly as it began. Plonczynski, after having been punched in the face, had tackled Spider to the ground making sure that as the two landed Spider was on the bottom and that it was Spider that took the force of both of them falling onto the cement pavement of the street. Spider wasn't injured so much as it dazed him a little, however that time it took for him to recover was all Plonczynski and his back-up needed to rush in and handcuffed him. As the handcuffing was completed, and Spider was being walked to a caged marked car,

Sniper and his mother arrived on scene. The other gang members had been pulled out of the car and searched as more units arrived, however it was Sniper that Plonczynski would now have to deal with. Spider's mother spoke almost no English, or never let on to law enforcement that she did which was a very common ploy just as much back then as it is today. Sniper was extremely upset, however he was calm and after explaining who he was and how he was related to Spider, he demanded to know exactly what his brother had done to land him in the back of a patrol car. As Plonczynski looked at him, he noticed that Sniper was wearing nothing but the color blue. From his blue collared shirt, to his blue jeans, to his blue sneakers, there was nothing to indicate that Sniper wasn't a full representative of the gang at this point. It was a little strange that Plonczynski hadn't yet met Sniper, especially given the fact that he was the brother to one of the most well-known gang members, and the brother to a gang leader. During this time, it was Plonczynski's job to explain everything. Neither of these children were related to the gang members in the car and thus their parents had to be contacted and asked if they knew where their children were and who they had permission to be with. This is not the kind of situation children of that age should have been ever allowed to witness or much less be a part of. Back then, or in today's world, putting children in danger such as that is a coward's act, but gang members often don't think with their heads or as rational people sometimes do. Sniper's mother had numerous questions about her other son Spider. She wanted to talk to him and she had wanted him released immediately. Of course, she was shouting this in Spanish and therefore it was up to Sniper to translate this to Plonczynski. Plonczynski had just gone one-on-one with the gang leader, where the gang leader refused to take verbal direction and listen to law enforcement and conduct himself as he was being ordered to do when he lawfully had a warrant out for his arrest. However, it was very telling of what kind of person Sniper was. It was amazing to Plonczynski, that as angry as Sniper and his mother were, Sniper was restrained and almost calculating in a way that he spoke and maintained his composure. Back then is no different than today and most gang members don't have that ability. He made no actions to make law enforcement think that he was a threat but by the same token, at the time he had never been patted down either. In today's world, this is a blunder that potentially could have had enormous implications. As we sit here today writing this book, law enforcement is at an all-time high for a number of attacks and ambushes by various different groups such as gangs. The danger in today's world is no less than the dangers back then and by every right Sniper should have been treated as if he was a threat. However, he was not treated that way. Plonczynski continued to talk to him calmly, cooly, and respectfully, even though he was bleeding from his nose ever so slightly, and sweating profusely. Sniper had numerous questions for Plonczynski, both from what his mother was asking him to repeat to Plonczynski as well as having his own. Plonczynski did his best to answer as many questions as he could, but neither Sniper nor his mother wanted to listen to the facts. The facts were very simple: Spider had a warrant, he was ordered out of the car, and refused to follow verbal direction, thus obstructing Plonczynski and other law enforcement from performing of their duties, then committed the heinous crime of battery on a law enforcement officer when he sucker punched Plonczynski. The gang members were allowed to leave with the juveniles in the end and did so. The K-9 handler followed the marked unit with Spider in the back of the cage to the district to office. This left Plonczynski alone with Sniper and his mother. Once again, in today's world, this would not fly, but back then law enforcement still could get by on the old adage "one riot one Ranger." Plonczynski did his best to try and explain things however, the mother wasn't taking any of his answers at face value and was demanding more and more answers. After a while Plonczynski became tedious of the situation and it was best to explain that there would be a bond, and they could bond him out after all of the charges had been made. Plonczynski then turned around and went to his car, while in the background listening to Snipers mother ranting and raving in Spanish. Plonczynski drive off shocked how calm Sniper had been. Sniper didn't raise his voice or make any comments other then those he translated for his mother. Plonczynski didn't know at the time, but he just met a gang member whom he would later arrest for possession of an automatic firearm, for attempted murder with several victims involved, and finally, racketeering. Plonczynski also didn't know that as calm as Sniper had been in this situation, it would become abundantly clear in the future that this gang member had a Jekyll and Hyde mentality, which all too often in law enforcement can lead to a law enforcement officer's complacency and then potentially to his injury or worse.

7 Intervention

The criminal justice system's goal is to keep citizens who are not a menace to society free in their communities to be productive citizens. With many initiatives such as courts designed to keep offenders out of jail and acquire the assistance to resolve whatever issue they may have (i.e. Drug Court, Prostitute Court, etc.), various legal systems with manpower, monies, and less than usual bureaucratic agendas throughout the country have taken a holistic approach. What happens to youth who join a gang? Prior to the suppression phase, intervention should be initiated and target the youth most at jeopardy for sustained involvement in gangs. Intervention programs conceptually appeal to most, however the data is limited and evaluating the efficacy is at best circumspect. What is posited as a good way forward is to examine the comparative risk of youth who are receiving prevention and intervention services with a similar sample of youth from the general population who are not. Successful prevention and intervention programs are important to stem the tide of gang involvement.

The reality is that when youth join a gang they are attracted by the allure (money, power, and respect) they think it brings. Once in, they feed off the excitement and adrenaline, becoming hooked. It is hard for most intervention programs to dissuade youth who have been brainwashed by the gang life. One of the issues with personnel in these programs is that they have not lived the life and thus the youth cannot relate to them nor do they want to. So how do you bridge this gap?

A successful gang intervention program adopts a holistic approach and meets gang members where they are. Former gang members are the best advocates because of their experience in the gang life which assists them in influencing youth still involved in the gang life. The former gang members have reformed by various means and have embraced abiding by the norms of society and thus can be emulated by current gang members that embrace their interventionist message. If these interventionists are funded then sometimes bureaucratic agendas dictate their actions. This becomes a balancing act for all involved and often results in failure. These interventionists balance the middle between the gangs and law enforcement and information sharing regarding the youth they serve. It's a catch-22 where they are expected to cooperate with law enforcement and divulge any information gleaned which may undermine trust of the community and those they are trying assist. If former gang members are able to work freely without interference while ensuring current gang members are not promoting further criminal acts, then you should have successful results.

Interventionist's goals are to mentor socio-economically challenged youth in their communities and connect them with vital resources to provide hope for the youth. The Chicago Area Project comes to mind, then the community unifying efforts were in the 1930s. Project initiatives targeted youth gangs with case managers who worked with them on the streets—meeting them in their homes, at their schools, and in local hangouts, per Klein (1995). Those involved assisted with employment opportunities and other activities positive in nature to foster appropriate decision making. Mentoring was crucial to this approach, which focused on strengthening the bonds connecting youth to the community (Krisberg & Austin, 1993), such as commitments to family, employment, and education. These bonds are crucially important as informal controls that prevent delinquency (Hirschi, 1969). This establishes the stability that facilitates criminal desistance (Laub & Sampson, 2003).

The Chicago Area Project developed indigenous leadership to administer local social programs (Krisberg & Austin, 1993), and gang intervention programs commonly utilize this model by hiring former gang members as interventionists. This experience gives interventionists a specialized knowledge of the lived realities of local youth (Martinez, 2003). Included in this is an understanding of the significance that street cultures have in shaping the identities of many of the young people they work with (Anderson, 2000; McDonald, 2003; Mendoza-Denton, 2008). Interactions with authority figures who criticize their style choices can be belittling experiences for young people, reinforcing their identification with the resistant subculture (Dance, 2002; Flores-Gonzalez, 2002). So meeting them where they are was understood in the 1930s and still rings true today.

8 Second Contact

Hugo and Carlos

It was in December 2005 when Plonczynski and his partner were driving around one afternoon in the city of Bradenton. As they drove a call had gone out for shots fired. The deputy that had been in the city's jurisdiction had been sitting in a church parking lot at approximately 7th Avenue and 15th St., East when he had heard the gunshots. He looked over his left shoulder and saw two Hispanic males riding bikes. The suspects were both pedaling as hard as they could when he had seen them. As both of the suspects were peddling one had his hands up in the air and the deputy was able to see what appeared to be a black handgun in the suspect's hand. He then gave chase and turned onto 7th Ave., East chasing them. One of the suspects believed to be Carlos cut right and fled the area. The deputy gave chase of the remaining suspect who turned out to be Hugo. Once on 17th St., Hugo went to a certain two-story house that was blue in color. There in the front yard he dumped the bike and began to run around the house. However the deputy was right on his tail. The deputy exited his vehicle and drew his firearm on Hugo. He then ordered Hugo numerous times to put the gun down and to walk over to him. Hugo, being the gang member that he is, elected not to comply with the verbal commands of the deputy and instead slowly walked around to the backyard only out of eyesight of the deputy for one second. He then returned to the front yard where he then walked over to the deputy empty-handed. It was at this point that 2 to 3 adult males came out of the house. The deputy took the suspect and handcuffed him immediately. Once done he had been handcuffed and was patted down in a huge bulge was felt in his right cargo pocket. It was shortly thereafter the Plonczynski and his partner showed up. Not having been here more than once, they were unaware of the significance of the location. This was actually a gang leader's house in the 17th St. clique of Sur 13. The 2 to 3 males that came outside had all been members of the gang. They were both well known to Hugo, but at this time they were not known to law enforcement. Once Plonczynski and his partner had showed up several other marked Sheriff's Office vehicles showed up as well. Hugo was taken out of the car and searched once again and a bag full of small caliber ammunition was found on his person. Deputies attempted to contact Hugo's mother, however no contact was made at this point. Hugo was read his Miranda rights, but true to form refused to talk to law enforcement. The ammunition was counted and there turned out to be 93 individual rounds. A B.O.L.O. went out for the second subject who was stopped a short ways away. It turned out to be Carlos. Carlos was wearing gang colors and was compliant with all law enforcement commands. No contraband was found on him and was shortly released thereafter. Unbeknownst to law enforcement these were old-time gang members, who had been in the system several times, and had been told their rights numerous times, both by law enforcement and by defense attorneys. Plonczynski and his partner both attempted to de-escalate the situation by talking to the males and explaining what had occurred. The residents were having none of it. They believed that law enforcement was doing nothing less than harassing a young man in front of his home. Plonczynski and his partner tried to explain that it was a school day during school hours and that both he and Carlos. Being true to form these gang members still were verbally combative and didn't care what law enforcement had to say. Moreover, they refused to allow law enforcement onto the property to search for the firearm even though law enforcement had every right to search for the missing handgun. As Plonczynski and his partner talked more and more, or at least tried to explain the situation to the residents, it became extremely clear that these were gang members. All of the subjects that exited the home had been wearing blue from head to toe and in one case had a blue bandanna hanging out of his back pocket. Plonczynski's partner had been in the Gang Unit much longer than him and was well versed at recognizing gang membership. He explained to Plonczynski that the blue bandanna that he had observed in the back pocket of one of the men that had exited the house had a certain type of pattern on it that was only used by one gang in all of Manatee County, and that gang was Sur 13. This made sense to Plonczynski. Hugo was already well documented and known to be a criminal street gang member in Sur 13. Coupled with the fact that Carlos was also a gang member in Sur 13 it now made sense why Hugo had come to this house. It was not Plonczynski's nor his partner's place to tell the deputy what to do in regard to recovering the firearm. When this happened Carlos was only 14 years old and Hugo barely 15. The only charge that the deputy was able to make against Hugo since the firearm was never recovered was obstruction of an officer without violence, a misdemeanor in Florida law. The charges were *nolle prossed* in the end. This was the result as the deputy had been released from his trial subpoena because he was out of town on vacation during the time the speedy trial was scheduled. The speedy trial had not expired, however the charge was supposed to be refiled and the prosecution would resume accordingly. However, the state attorney's office never did refile those charges, and Hugo once again slipped through the cracks of justice and was able to resume the gang lifestyle. It is quite possible that because of the justice system failing as many times as it did with both Carlos and Hugo, that both of these juveniles learned the wrong lesson from the get-go. Had they been given a swift hand across their own from the justice system in the beginning, it is possible to believe that both of them might have had productive lives. However when this occurred in December 2005, once again the justice system would fail them, fail the community, and allow them to further their criminal gang lifestyles. It was never determined where Hugo had gotten the gun from or how he could've afforded it but in most likelihood the firearm was probably taken in a burglary that they both had committed sometime earlier that day while skipping school. This was just one more act, among numerous other criminal acts, that were destined to be part of the racketeering case that was later made against both of them.

In September 2009, Pieper was conducting juvenile curfew checks with Bradenton Police Department's Street Crimes Unit and Manatee County Juvenile Probation Officers. He would set up these operations once every two weeks. These operations were very simple to do and could generate great results for the community and the bosses. Every month the Juvenile Probation Supervisor would email Plonczynski and Pieper the current updated list of juvenile offenders who were on court ordered probation. The senior Juvenile Probation Officer was very proactive and passionate about her job so the operation was usually a go (Figure 8.1).

Pieper would call Plonczynski and discuss the worst offenders in the city and county and if Pieper was joining in the operation, he would then pick out the most violent and worst offenders and then, depending on the scale of the operation, the city's Gang Unit and Juvenile Probation Office would all load up in separate vehicles and go from residence to residence. Plonczynski had originally done large-scale juvenile probation checks of this nature from early on in 2003. It was called Operation: Door Knock. Once every 3 months or so, the Juvenile

Figure 8.1 Pieper and Plonczynski (AKA "Ski") Discuss an Arrest.

Probation Officers, City Police Department, and Sheriff's Deputies would conduct a "sweep" and check on 75–115 juveniles in one night to confirm that they were all in compliance with their court ordered curfews. By 2009, the Sheriff's Office had gotten away from this type of large-scale operation and now both the city and the county were doing smaller versions of these checks.

The operation was pretty simple at the core of it. If the juvenile was outside of their residence after his/her curfew without their parent or guardian, they would be in violation of the court ordered curfew and sanctions. If the juvenile was a gang member and was hanging out with other known gang members, then they were violating the court's order and the sanctions placed on them by the court and they could be arrested as well. If by chance the law enforcement officer checked on the juvenile and caught them committing a new crime (such as possession of narcotics), they would arrest them. On this occasion Pieper's team would not generally arrest on just the violation because it wasn't a new charge. As such, the juvenile would only be held a couple of hours until their parents or whomever they called for a ride would come and pick them up. However, if law enforcement obtained an arrest warrant (commonly referred to as a Juvenile Pickup Order) for the violation, then the juvenile would be held overnight until they could go in front of the judge in the morning. Often what Pieper would do is conduct curfew checks throughout the week and do little mini round-ups on Friday, that way the offenders would be off of the streets for the majority of the weekend. It was one way of keeping crime down on the weekends which can be the community's busiest time for calls for service.

On this particular night, Pieper was in a vehicle with a supervisor. As they were pulling into an apartment complex called City Walk, Pieper advised him that Hugo had been staying in an apartment with another Sureno gang member at this location. Pieper was really just making small talk as they were there to check on two other offenders who were on probation for their role in a triple homicide in Orange County. As they pulled in, a very large black woman began yelling at them, "He's over there, he's over there. He punched me and stole my phone!" None of them had any clue as to what she was talking about as they had not been dispatched to a 911 call. One of the officers that they were with agreed to see what the incident was regarding and Pieper and the supervisor continued the checks. Pieper and the supervisor went to the location where a juvenile was supposed to be located at. Pieper knocked on the door several times with no answer. As they were waiting in the parking lot for the officers who went to go and see about the possible robbery to return to the scene, the two juveniles Pieper was checking on arrived in a car with their mother. Even though it was after their court ordered curfew they were not in violation because they were with their mother.

A short time later, the other officers returned and one had stated that they were walking back from talking to patrol units and he smelled marijuana being smoked from a first-floor apartment patio. Moreover, there was a large crowd there. This officer then pointed to the apartment where Hugo had been living. The decision was made to further investigate this law violation as it was a known gang hang out. Officers quietly approached the apartment and as they did so it became very apparent that the crowd was still out on the patio smoking marijuana. All this was very evident based on the smell and the fact that the persons on the patio were coughing and spitting on the ground. As they got closer, Pieper was able to look through a break in the 10-foot privacy fence that surrounded the patio. To no surprise, Pieper saw Hugo wearing a black and blue plaid shirt. Pieper didn't actually see him with the marijuana but he could still smell it.

During this time, communities statewide were having a lot of home invasions where the suspects were identifying themselves as police officers. Our jurisdiction was also having this same problem. In knowing just how violent Hugo and his fellow Surenos were, the officers had to be careful on how they identified themselves, especially because they didn't know who else was on the patio or in the apartment. Pieper decided to say, "Hey Hugo it's Pieper, it's Pieper, it's Pieper," as he had been dealing with Hugo for several years and he didn't want him to think this was a robbery. As Pieper was looking through the crack in the fence he saw Hugo open the sliding glass door to the apartment and everyone began to run inside. Pieper then opened the gate to the fence and observed several of the subjects running toward the front door where another officer had decided to set up. Pieper quickly advised over the radio that they were coming his way. Just then, one of the gang members opened the front door and one of the officers yelled, "I have drugs in plain view!" At that time, the supervisor along with several other officers and Pieper made entry to the apartment through the sliding glass door. They noticed several younger males and females running toward the back bedrooms of the apartment as they did so. One of the other officers began ordering all the subjects in the living room to the ground at gun point. As Pieper was walking through the living room he noticed the marijuana blunt that they were smoking still burning on the carpet next to one of the several well-known gang members that were present.

Pieper then walked over to Hugo who was now on both knees with his hands up behind his head. Pieper asked him if he had anything illegal on him and Hugo replied, "Yes." In disbelief, Pieper looked at him and asked what he had and where it was. Hugo then stated that he had a gun in the waistband of his pants. Being a very dangerous moment when a law enforcement officer is confronted with a gang member with a gun, Pieper quickly took Hugo's hands, placed them behind his back, and detained him in handcuffs. As Pieper was doing this he looked right near Hugo's knees and noticed a very large bag of marijuana. He asked Hugo if the marijuana was his and he said, "Yes, but it's for personal use."

As all of this was going on, the scene supervisor and the other officers went into the back bedrooms and recovered six or seven younger juvenile subjects, all of whom were documented gang members or associates per Florida State Statute and definition. Once all the individuals in the apartment were secured in handcuffs, Pieper recovered a six shooter revolver from Hugo's waistband that looked as if it was located on a sunken pirate ship from the 1200s. It truly appeared to be an old pirate's gun. Pieper looked at Hugo and said, "Hugo, what the hell is this? Where did you get this fucking thing?" Pieper then stated that he expected more style in his firearms choices from Hugo, as a joke. Here was a hardcore gang member with gang tattoos on his face, carrying the most awkward gun one could ever think to see on a gang member. It took Pieper about 25 minutes to get this gun unloaded. At one point Hugo leaned over to Pieper and said, "Hey Pieper, just take the cuffs off and I'll unload it for you." Pieper looked at Hugo like he was crazy and said, "Hugo, I'm not going to take you out of handcuffs and put a loaded gun in your hands." He couldn't believe he would even suggest such a thing although, at the time, Pieper did appreciate Hugo's courtesy as this gun was kicking his ass on how to unload it. Later, Pieper was able to get the gun cleared and rendered safe (very much later).

By the time officers were done at the apartment, Hugo was arrested for possession of marijuana with intent to distribute. The total weight of the marijuana was over 190 grams. Hugo was also under arrest for carrying a concealed firearm. At the time of this arrest Hugo was not a convicted felon. Due to this incident though, several arrests took place. Two other subjects in the apartment were also arrested for outstanding warrants. During the prosecution phase of this case for Hugo, a gang prosecution Assistant State Attorney was assigned to the case. This one was a very good and aggressive prosecutor. One day Pieper was in her office talking about the charges. She felt that the state couldn't charge Hugo for the gun charge because Hugo was in a place that the state considered to be his residence and he wasn't a convicted felon. After further discussion with an office chief, it was agreed that the charge didn't fit.

Pieper and the prosecutor went back to her office to continue talking about the case. As they sat there, Pieper and the prosecutor began to talk about their options and any other charges that could be filed. Pieper recommended charging "persons engaged in criminal offences having a firearm." She looked at Pieper and reached for her statute book, looked it up, and said, "Ben, why didn't you bring this up before?" in a loud voice. She then picked up the phone and called the office's chief prosecutor. She explained to him the situation and Pieper could hear him say, "Why didn't he say that when you guys were over here?" in a loud voice. The state agreed to amend the charge and issue a warrant for Hugo as he had already bonded out on the original charges.

About two weeks later, Plonczynski saw Hugo at the court house. He knew about the warrant and arrested him in a court room. Needless to say Hugo was less than thrilled and calmly issued Ski several threats advising him that this arrest was total crap and Ski had better watch his back. It wasn't the first time Ski had been threatened by a high-ranking gang member and it wasn't the last. So like many times in the past, Ski documented the threat and got Hugo to the jail. Ski didn't reply at the time to any of Hugo's threats. It wasn't really his style. Hugo wasn't able to bail out this time as the bail was pretty high. Due to the fact that he was not a convicted felon, everyone believed that the state probably was not going to get any prison time out of this arrest. In working with this prosecutor, the state was able to get Hugo to plea to nine months county jail and adjudicated guilty on both counts.

Now Hugo was a convicted felon. It took us a lot of years to figure out and get the prosecutors on board with setting these guys up for the future. Hugo was one of the many issues both Ski and Pieper had to contend with. This one case though was a bench mark for a case that was yet to come. Hugo was a hardcore gang member in Sur 13. What he didn't know yet was that Ski and Pieper were already working with FDLE, the Statewide Prosecutors Office and several other agencies to charge Sur 13 members with the Racketeer Influenced and Corrupt Organizations Act. It was a law made for this very group that in the coming months and years would change the criminals, the community, and law enforcement that worked the case.

Oso

Manatee County is broken up into several jurisdictions in law enforcement, and while gang members rarely consider what law enforcement jurisdiction they are living in, it can literally make or break a criminals career depending on what law enforcement agency is most prevalent or holds the jurisdiction of where that gang member resides. Originally, Oso was arrested in West Palm Beach as a gang member for a gang related murder. Since he was tried as a juvenile he served little time for such a heinous crime. After his release from juvenile prison, he was released back on the streets where he basked in the street credibility of having been a murderer for the gang. There is no higher respect for a gang member then to have killed for the gang. It is the pinnacle in street credibility and respect. Originally "Spanky" who was a gang member in Manatee County Florida was in West Palm Beach and had met oh so there. Law enforcement came across the two together and conducted a field interview report showing the association between the two. Also present during this encounter was Oso's girlfriend who is a documented member of the criminal street gang MS 13. What transpired between the three of them during those days in West Palm Beach law enforcement will never know. However what is known is that all three of them would later move to and live in Manatee County Florida. It was probably seen as a fresh start for Oso and his girlfriend. For many years he had had a deal with law enforcement in West Palm Beach knew him well and had known what atrocities against the community he had been a part of. The first time that he came across law enforcement, would be on a street where both the city's jurisdiction in law enforcement and the counties jurisdiction in law enforcement split the north side of the street the city held as part of their jurisdiction the south side belong to the county. It was on a regular day of work that Ben Pieper came across both "Spanky" and "Oso". Pieper being a intelligent gang investigator, new that someone who is in the company of Spanky, who was also wearing all blue in all likelihood was also a gang member. However in this case, it was a gang member the Pieper had never encountered before. When gang investigators have been on the job for as much time as both Plonczynski and Pieper had been at that time seeing new faces that they could not identify was a red flag. After a while a good investigator will know just about everybody who's in the game when it comes to gangs and while no investigator can no every gang member, it's very rare when you have investigated them as long and as diligently as both Plonczynski and Pieper had that someone new pops up, unknown in all respects, as was the case here. Pieper got out of his car and conducted a consensual encounter. What transpired next would lead to several investigations and ultimately to the downfall of Oso's criminal career as a gang member in Manatee County for quite some time. After Pieper got out of the car and quickly realized the street was the dividing line between the city's jurisdiction and the that of the county. Pieper watched as both bangers exited a local corner store that was in Bradentons jurisdiction. They were both covered head to toe in Sur 13 gang attire wearing blue and black with bandannas hanging out of their back pockets. Pieper knew that they were heavily intoxicated as they swayed in their walk. They then began to walk across the street to their house which was in Ski's jurisdiction. Pieper and his team quickly made contact with Oso and Spanky stopping them in the center of the street. Pieper had dealt with Spanky in the past. True to form when Pieper asked Spanky for consent to search his person, Spanky told him to "pound sand". Oso stood there quietly at first not knowing Pieper or his team. As Pieper and Spanky were going round for round in a verbal "debate", Oso finally decided it would be a good idea to pipe up and speak. Oso who was so intoxicated that he could barely stand. As such, he decided that this would be a good time to become verbally abusive towards law enforcement. Pieper and Oso stodd toe to toe in the center of the street while Oso spewed insult after insult. Professionalism is a hard thing to keep in check in these situations, however Pieper knew (as most law enforcement often does) that while today the bad guy may win a battle, lady justice often wins the war. In this encounter Oso admitted to being a Sur 13 gang member, as he insulted everything he could about Pieper and his team, but gave Pieper and his team a false name.

After the encounter, Pieper was hot. He called Plonczynski in a excited stated and couldn't speak fast enough to explain what had just happened. Ski quickly started looking in to the situation and began making phone calls.

After Plonczynski and Pieper had learned the identity of Oso, Plonczynski went back and started doing his homework. He researched all of the history in police reports that he could find from any jurisdiction he could find them from. In doing so he also pulled a criminal history and saw that Oso had been arrested and convicted of murder. This murder had been during Oso's juvenile years and as such he was tried as a juvenile. During the plea agreement for the murder, the state agreed to a downward departure from the mandatory sentencing and as such Oso was given what would be considered a slap on the wrist for murder. However, even though he was convicted as a juvenile under Florida state law he was still considered a felon until 24 years old. Oso still fit into this category. Plonczynski was able to obtain court records to prove the felony conviction and the adjudication making him a felon by law.

Plonczynski went further and pulled all recent reports with Oso and checked to see if he had registered as a felon in the county with the Sheriff's Office as he was required to do so by law. After a thorough investigation, it was determined that Oso had not made any notification whatsoever to any law enforcement agency, or any other agencies such as the Department of Highway Safety and Motor Vehicles that he was now living in Manatee County. Plonczynski contacted both his people and Bradenton's Gang Unit and explained that as a result of his investigation, he had sought an arrest warrant for Oso for the violation of not registering as a felon in the county. This warrant would not violate any sort of probation and didn't hold a significant amount of jail time if a conviction was obtained. It was only a misdemeanor not to register. It would allow investigators to learn more about Oso though, and in the gang world, money isn't usually put aside for bond or lawyers, rather it's spent on drugs and partying. As such, even small charges can lead to long durations in jail.

Once Plonczynski had gotten the warrant signed by the court and entered into FCIC, he notified all law enforcement of the warrant and put out a "be on the lookout" or B.O.L.O. as is referred to. It would be Pieper that would ultimately find Oso along with another criminal street gang member from Manatee County.

While driving by Oso's residence Pieper noticed Oso and another gang member hanging out across the street. Pieper knew of the active warrant for Oso. Pieper and his team made contact with Oso and the other gang member. During this encounter, Oso was very polite and professional with Pieper (as this time he was not intoxicated). Pieper informed Oso of his warrant and placed him in handcuffs. During a search of Oso, Pieper located a small bag of marijuana in his pocket.

Pieper took Oso to his satellite office to process and interview him. Once at Pieper's office he began to talk to Oso in length. Post-Miranda, Oso stated that he was a member of Sur 13 from West Palm Beach. Oso agreed to let Pieper take pictures of him and all of his tattoos. Oso had "just a dream" tattooed across his back which indicated his set name from West Palm Beach.

Pieper called Plonczynski and informed him of the incident. Plonczynski was happy to learn that Oso had been arrested and it was in the company of another gang member who just so happened to be the brother of "Spanky." Pieper informed Plonczynski that Oso was in possession of a small amount of marijuana and that he had charged him with that as well. Plonczynski, who had been looking at possibly doing another R.I.C.O. arrest wave, asked Pieper why he charged Oso with the marijuana instead of holding it as an open or substantive charge for a R.I.C.O. Pieper simply had chosen to make the charge on the marijuana sooner rather than later. Pieper stated that he had charged him "by accident." In truth, Pieper had just felt it was more important to get as much jail time in on Oso as possible. It was a rookie move by a seasoned vet. This incident would lead to much ribbing by Plonczynski as the years went by and a fact that Plonczynski still reminds Pieper of to this day.

As a result of Pieper's diligence in locating and arresting Oso, along with the other gang member that he was with, investigators were able to listen to jail calls and observe visitations, as they are recorded in the jail. This gave investigators solid intelligence as to who the associates of Oso currently were and who they dealt with primarily in the gang. Oso didn't have much to begin with while living in Manatee County and while his girlfriend worked diligently at the outlet mall, the money that she made was needed to pay for rent, food, electricity, water, and all of the things that go along with having to survive with children. As such, Oso got little money while he was in jail and did not have enough to bond out immediately. Through further investigation Plonczynski learned of an aggravated battery that occurred at the gang house whereby one of the gang's female members brought over another girl who she worked with to hang out, drink some beers, and smoke some weed. This girl, not being a gang member and not knowing anything about gangs or what takes place in their presence, had no idea what was going to happen when she went over to the house and just thought that she was going over to party and have a good time. Most members of society will never know how alien gang member's lives are to the rest of the community. These gang members don't live like the rest of us. Their moral compass is far off from the normal patterns that one would see with an everyday member of society. This we know is not okay. Oso thought it was okay to murder and to flaunt his gang membership. Oso believed that he could yell at law enforcement, the way he yelled at Pieper and fellow officers during the first encounter he had been involved in with law enforcement in Manatee County.

During the party, Oso and another gang member attempted to sexually assault this non-gang-related female after there had been some consumption of alcohol and probably drugs. When she resisted their advances things became physical. One gang member grabbed her and placed her in a headlock, while the other one repeatedly punched her. She began screaming and attempted to fight her way out of the headlock. While she was still in the headlock she was punched repeatedly in the face and body but was able to scrape, claw, and bite her way out, and she fled to the street. As luck would have it, there was a marked Sheriff's Office cruiser patrolling down the street that she was able to flag down for help. She explained what had taken place and the deputy called for backup. An investigation was started into what had occurred, but as none of the gang members would cooperate and corroborate what occurred, nor would her coworker, who stated that nothing had happened and that the victim was merely drunk and high, no charges and arrests were made. Plonczynski obtained the report and followed up with the victim who is now at a different job in part as a result of what occurred that evening. She didn't want to be around the coworker who knew what had occurred, or allow the gang to find her after having made the report against them. Plonczynski interviewed the victim at length over the phone where it became extremely clear to him that she was scared of what had happened and even more scared of what potentially could occur in the future should she agree to testify against them at a later time as a result of this incident. She had gone into the house just to have a good time and quickly learned that when regular members of society mix with gang members whose moral compass is far off from their own, sometimes bad things happen and sometimes tragic things happen. Plonczynski wasn't able to make charges in this case against anyone who was present that day for what occurred, and Oso is still the main suspect in that case which is still open to this day. Neither Oso nor law enforcement knew it yet, but things were about to transpire in the not so distant future that would have a significant impact on his career as a criminal street gang member and show his association was stronger with the gang than local investigators had known of to that point.

Javier

Some time after Javier had been arrested for murder, gone to trial, and was convicted he moved on to the prison system which would be his home for the rest of his natural born life. In 2009, Javier was housed in the Indian River Correctional Facility in Florida and it was during this time that a "kite" was located by corrections officers at the prison. This "kite" was addressed to an inmate by the name of "Chucky" who is known to the correction staff there to be a member of the gang Sur 13. In this letter there were two different forms of handwriting and it was quite clear to investigators that this letter was meant to be passed on with two messages. The first portion of the letter was written by "Lil Chapo." This person was known to be the second in command in all the Florida Department of Corrections of Sur 13. In order to determine who had written the other half of the kite, investigators went back to find out who the roommate was for "Lil Alex." Upon doing the research, investigators realized that the roommate was Javier. Javier was known to investigators in the Florida Department of Corrections as the current crown of Sur 13. After reviewing Javier's handwriting and matched it to the writing on the kite, it was determined that Javier was the actual author of the other portion of the letter.

On the front page inmate Javier is telling inmate "Chucky" to "be true to that blue" and "to tell his carnals that he loves them and to keep it real and am still holding this bitch down." Inmate Javier then gives nicknames of his "carnals."

On the back page inmate Javier listed the following nicknames of four individuals and then provided their real names:

Grim   *******
Kreepz   *******
Dough Boy   *******
OutCold   ********

Inmate Javier then stated, "These the nigga that snitched on me let the carnals know."

The corrections personnel were able to locate all of the individuals listed with the exception of Grim. He had not been transported yet from the jail. It was apparent that inmate Javier was ordering a "hit" against these four inmates. The letter or "kite" was not delivered to the intended inmate, but it was unknown if inmate Javier succeeded at ordering hits with previous letter "kites."

Inmate Javier was currently in disciplinary confinement for two separate gang-related activity charges, one being for recruiting. Inmate Javier is scheduled to be released from disciplinary confinement in May 20**. Inmate Javier received a third disciplinary report on March of that year, for gang-related activity regarding this current letter "kite."

Inmate Javier posed a risk to security and other inmates. It was apparent by his actions that he had no respect for the rules of the institution. Inmate Javier has made it clear that he intends to continue his gang activities no matter the consequences. Inmate Javier needs to be reviewed for Case Management status, this way he will not pose a threat to security or the safety of other inmates.

Javier still, to this day, is a "Crown" in the Florida DOC. He is a threat to all and orders are made by him that affect both the prison population all over the state and out on the streets. Rumor has it that both Plonczynski and Pieper have been "Green Lit" by Javier. This fact was confirmed in part by a Homicide Detective in the Manatee County Sheriff's Office during an interview he had with another gang member in prison some time later.

9   Sustained Programs

Historical philosophies of criminal justice reform have been tried and implemented multiple times over the past few centuries. Criminal justice theories and the work of theorists have set the standard for many initiatives. These theories and proposals for criminal justice transformation are still impacting the criminal justice system today. To address the need for shifts in our society, there needs to be change in criminal justice and this transformation is evident in criminal justice reform.

A critical part of this initiative was to tackle the disparities among various sub-groups and create equity, access, and quality (Dollarhide & Lemberger, 2006; Gardiner, Canfield-Davis, & Anderson, 2009; Grey, 2010; Hanushek & Rivkin, 2010; Harrison-Jones, 2007; Hess, 2006; Imazeki, & Reschovsky, 2004; LaRuth, 2005; Menken, 2009; Murnane & Papay, 2010). Arce et al. (2005), Steffan (2004), Yell, Katsiyannas, and Shiner (2006), debated the effectiveness of gang prevention and the extent to which it addressed the purpose for which it was intended. More recently, other government proposed programs were instituted to help the criminal justice system compete with other nations' effectiveness in countering gangs.

There are other approaches that help gang members and other people who have been radicalized. One such organization is called ExitUSA, www.exitusa. org. They have other programs that help former gang members www.lifeafterhate. org/#!programs/c21kz—another is Harmony through Hockey. It helps children in Philadelphia learn hockey, who otherwise would not be able to afford it. It teaches them discipline and respect: two key components gang members reported as rational for joining the gang in the first place.

Brzenchek interviewed an Arizona public school teacher who has a number of gangs in their classroom. They wanted to remain anonymous due to their own safety and they stated, "Our public schools along the US-MX border are infected by gangsta glamour. Having taught both in Southern Texas and Arizona I've acquired countless anecdotes to attest to this statement. Otherwise notorious figures in the cartels are idealized by teens and tweens as modern-day Robin Hoods. Critically, our own children are now exposed to a societal disease that they would naturally not be exposed to if schools had more leeway to screen enrollments. Surely, living in a third world country in fear for your lives daily is a great motivator to side with the presiding power and/or to flee. Today I witness both. Acquiring the [gangster] lifestyle and fleeing undetected to greener pastures [America].

The prevalence of gangs will undoubtedly spread unless measures are taken to root what has grown in our soil and additional efforts are made to prevent infected cells from attaching themselves to the host."

Brzenchek then met in Annapolis, Maryland with Tony Fowler who works as a liaison for the US Department of Education in Washington, DC. This informal meeting in 2015 was to update on SMART—Strengthening the Mid-Atlantic Region for Tomorrow initiatives. Brzenchek was appointed recently by Bob Carullo (Executive Director of SMART) as the Deputy Chair for the Homeland Security Group. In this role Brzenchek participated in the Democratic National Committee for a bi-partisan effort on school safety. Brzenchek focuses on school safety issues such as gangs and emergency management as a part of his llc: All Source International Security; www.allsourceinternationalsecurity.com which is a member of SMART. During this meeting Mr. Fowler and Brzenchek engaged in a conversation regarding Brzenchek's PhD research on gangs and presentations throughout the country to include such challenged areas as Los Angeles, Chicago, Dallas, DC, Orlando, Philadelphia, and his hometown of Wilkes Barre, Pennsylvania. Mr. Fowler mentioned some tremendous initiatives regarding drug abuse he is involved within the DMV—DC, Maryland, and Virginia areas and both agreed there was some crossover with gangs. All present agreed that a gang centric presentation should be coordinated in the DMV area to raise awareness. Prior to the conclusion of the meeting Mr. Fowler was gracious enough to provide Brzenchek with a portfolio that contained information on the great work The Harmony Project is doing. Dr. Martin, the founder of the Harmony Project, started the program and later got the attention of Dr. Nina Kraus, who then began to study the brain development of the students involved in the program. The Harmony Project and Youth Development through the Arts was founded in Los Angeles, California.

According to Dr. Martin who is the Harmony Project Founder (2009), "we take at-risk youth whose families earn less than 185% of the federal poverty and give them musical instruments (such as violins, cellos, flutes, clarinets, trumpets, etc.) and year-round-tuition-free music lessons, and we build neighborhood youth orchestras with these kids after school hours and on Saturdays." The Harmony Project enrolls kids early in elementary school on through graduating from high school and they have a scholarship to assist students' transition into higher education. The dropout rates improved from 50% for the demographic that makes up the Harmony Project enrollment, yet 100% of Harmony Project students remain enrolled in school. The bottom line the program impact is: keep kids safe in school and out of trouble; improve kids' school performance, behavior and mood; develop personal discipline, strategic thinking, time-management, focus, commitment, and task-persistence; help kids get along better with others and at home (through performing in ensembles and youth orchestras); and help parents learn to better support their kids and reduce family dysfunction (through ongoing parent education programs).

Brzenchek is from the Northeastern Pennsylvania region and has been involved on varying fronts because of erosion of communities within it due to gangs. In his proactive involvement with law enforcement and other stakeholders, Operation

Gang Up was mentioned as a robust gang initiative. According to the Operation Gang Up website it has its roots in early 2011 when U.S. Representative Lou Barletta (R) and State Senator John Yudichak (D) came together to discuss the increasing gang activity in Northeastern Pennsylvania, and how to combat the growing issue. As early as 2005, Mr. Barletta and Hazleton Police Chief Robert Ferdinand recognized problems with gangs and traveled to Washington, DC to meet with officials in the Department of Justice. They believed the first step of this new project would be to promote gang awareness and educate the public on gang-related topics. The primary purpose and goals of the operation include working closely with local law enforcement as well as community administrators and educators to develop preventative strategies, conduct research and institute the best practices for reducing gang activity, and offer training to those who require it. Special Agent Dones of the F.B.I.'s Behavioral Analysis Unit at the Gang Awareness Seminar at Penn State Hazleton in 2012 called gangs "urban terrorists" who are constantly moving into communities and recruiting new members from all walks of life, including the military, to build "empires" and become well known. He said there are a varying array of 30,000-plus gangs in every corner of the United States, ranging from well-known groups to lesser-known or up-and-coming packs. Dones said gangs are not a problem associated with one specific ethnic group, race, or gender. In fact, he said, gangs once predominantly made up of one race or ethnic group are now accepting anyone, including women, into their group. This initiative is a prime example of how all stakeholders should work and share information together.

What really works? A family support structure. For this next topic of discussion we'll take a look into the effect of family; more specifically, the effect that mothers can have on gang members. When we talk about a gang member such as Hugo we have to take a look at how he became the hardened criminal that he is. The first time Pieper meet Hugo he asked him how old he was. Hugo replied with "thirteen plus one." Even at the young age of 14 he refused to say the number because the number "14" refers to his biggest rival Norte 14. Hugo was a strange type of hardcore gang member, or maybe he was brilliant. Over the course of about 15 years, Hugo had escaped felony prosecution; in many cases this is normal in the gang world because the victims of gang crimes usually don't follow through with the SAO or the DA depending on where they live because they're either rivals or scared of retaliation. Pieper had arrested Hugo no less than 15 times in about 10 years and that's not including Ski's arrests. So how did Hugo last so long without a felony conviction?

Simple, he was smart. I can say with 100% certainty that Hugo had never run from or fought Pieper. Over all the years of arrests, traffic stops, consensual encounters, and situations where Hugo was the victim of a crime he absolutely refused to cooperate but he wouldn't resist or obstruct an investigation. Name, rank, and date of birth is all that is required of POW's to give to their captors. Hugo would only answer the required questioning for the proper arrest paperwork. If you tried to slide in a question about the surrounding circumstances he would just sit in his chair quietly. If the next question was specific to the arrest paperwork he would answer it. If you asked him about SPM (South Park Mexican) or football he would answer it, try to slide in a question about the case, and crickets.

If you work in law enforcement for long enough you begin to learn a great deal about the members of your community and their family members. In the world of gangs this is also true, but if you have the privilege of working gangs for long enough you almost build a special bond with the gang members and their families. You will be there when they're drunk and high as a kite at the ripe old age of 14, sorry thirteen plus one. You'll be there for the birth of most likely what will be several children, you'll be there when they get shot in the face just as Pieper was when Hugo and Carlos got caught slipping in rival gang territory. You may even be invited to their wedding as Ignacio Rivera invited Pieper to his. The bottom line is that when these kids start out in their gangbanging careers, you're going to be there with them right alongside their fellow gang members, mothers, and fathers.

Over the years Pieper and Ski had developed a very nice relationship with Maria, Hugo's mother. Maria was a very nice woman who loved Hugo and his two brothers very much. Dad was not in the picture but Maria did everything that she could to provide for the children. Every time Pieper and Ski would go to Maria's residence. Looking to arrest Hugo on an outstanding warrant, mom would answer the door and the first thing they would do is talk to her and ask he how she was doing. They would engage in conversation until Maria would ask, "What did Hugo do this time?" They would tell her and without hesitation she would turn over Hugo to them. Maria never got mad or upset at Pieper or Ski, she never questioned them, or gave them any kind of mouth or attitude. You see, Maria knew exactly what Hugo was doing out in the streets and she also knew that Pieper and Ski were just doing their jobs.

Hugo knew this as well. Pieper and Ski never harassed nor picked on Hugo but he was a very hardcore, violent, and a high-ranking Sur 13 gang member so there were times when Hugo did get some "special attention." Every time that Pieper and Ski went out with Hugo whether he was the victim/suspect of a crime or it was just a consensual encounter, they always made it a point to ask how Maria was doing. They took a special interest in an aspect of his life that was not gang related or work related in their case. Both Pieper and Ski knew that Maria was sick and had a lot of medical issues. In looking back it's clear that both Hugo and his mother recognized what Pieper and Ski were doing and it may have kept them safe when many other officers were getting death threats or "Green Lit" by gang members.

Even though Maria did everything she could to keep Hugo away from the gang it was a lost cause. She didn't let him have any friends over to the house, she refused to buy him blue clothing, and she worked diligently with law enforcement to keep him safe. In the end, Hugo was just mad at the world and there was nothing that could have been done.

In another example of a Sur 13 mom who started off being as supportive as she could and worked with law enforcement very much in the beginning turned out to be one of the biggest problems. Claudia was the mother of three of the most notorious gang members in Manatee County. Two sons and a daughter were founding members of the 17th St clique of Sur 13. Lil Bandit, Javier, and Cecilia were all about the same age, born with in a year or so of each other. In the beginning Lil Bandit was the most violent. From an early age he was directing the gang's activities and doing drive-by shootings. Javier was more calm and laid back but took more of an enforcer roll and he was the biggest and toughest. Cecilia was used to bait other rival gang members into certain situations and was also used as a recruiter to get other females into the gang. Cecilia was the youngest but was so hardcore that when Pieper went to arrest her on an outstanding warrant she ran into her house and hid her bandanna under her bed. Cecilia did this because in Florida we are able to seize profits, proceeds, or instrumentalities of criminal street gang involvement. Cecilia knew that Pieper would seize her bandanna and place it into evidence and use it to show that she is a gang member.

What Cecilia failed to hide under bed was a bag of marijuana that was in her pocket. Cecilia was so down for her gang that she would rather catch a new charge and get VOPed all on top of her warrant than lose another bandanna to Pieper. Getting back to Claudia, when the kids were all in 7th, 8th, and 9th grade Claudia was very proactive in working with Pieper and Ski in efforts to keep the kids away from the gang. Claudia would call Pieper and Ski directly and tell them where her kids were when she knew that they were looking for them. She would call to let them know when the kids were on probation and, when they were not in school or out past curfew. This was great for a while but like many parents, she got tired of Pieper and Ski dealing with her kids and always arresting them.

Instead of getting mad at her kids or cracking down on them and holding them accountable for their actions, she turned on Pieper and Ski. Claudia stopped calling and talking to them. This created a sense of empowerment with kids. All three kids felt like nothing could stop them and for a while they were right. Lil Bandit went away for a year because he caught a shooting charge, after that sightings and run-ins with him were few and far between. While Cecilia was out and about running wild on the streets, Javier found himself in a whole new kind of trouble. These guys were accustomed to getting arrested for shooting at rival gang members and going to the Juvenile Detention Facility and having to stay there for thirty days. After the thirty days was up, the state attorney's office had to drop the charges as the victims refused to cooperate. Well, one faithful afternoon Javier, Yoda, and a few of their associates got into a fight with some rival gang members. Javier decided to pull a gun and proceeded to shoot multiple rounds off into the crowed. Many times when this is done nobody gets hit or maybe a rival will get shot in the leg. This time an innocent 9-year-old kid got hit. Little Stacy Williams took a bullet while merely riding his bike.

Stacy was able to ride his bike to his grandmother's front door where he fell to his death on her door step. Ski was one of the many hard working investigators that night and called Pieper who rounded his team up and set up on Javier's house. Javier lived in Pieper's jurisdiction and was on probation with an 8:00 pm curfew. Once Pieper and his team were on scene they observed the suspect vehicle parked in front of Javier's residence and were positive that he was inside. Javier wasn't one to usually miss curfew, oddly enough. Once Ski and his team had a search warrant for the residence and an arrest warrant in hand they hit the house. As law enforcement went to the front door to arrest Javier, Ski went to handcuff Javier. Javier pulled away and told Ski to "get his fucking hands off of him." Investigators took Javier in to custody and then conducted the search warrant. It was one of the proudestest moments in Ski's career still to this day. At one point during the night Javier found himself in the back seat of a patrol vehicle with Yoda. A recorder was placed into the vehicle and the two engaged in conversation. Hoping to catch them talking about the murder, Javier told Yoda, "Don't worry, he was just a kid, we'll be out in 30 days."

Needless to say, Javier found himself charged with murder and all of his co-defendants rolled on him. Sur 13 gang members that were wrapped in Ski's R.I.C.O. case even flipped on him. It took the jury 4 hours to find Javier guilty of killing little Stacy Williams. At the sentencing hearing Claudia spoke on behalf of her son. Her words to the judge were, "If you give my boy life you'll be sorry, he did nothing wrong and should be set free." Ladies and gentlemen, when the mother is so naïve and hell bent on not helping her children by facing the issues, this is what happens. Javier is now the second highest ranking Sur 13 gang member in the Florida prison system.

These are two examples of mothers who loved their kids dearly, one continued to help law enforcement and the other chose not to. In both cases the outcome was the same, kids and young men being sent away to prison for extended amounts of time. What happens when the mom is a gang member herself? What happens when mom directs the gang's activities? Mariana was the mother of, once again, three hardcore gang members. Mr. Sancho was the oldest; he was a founding member of the Brown Pride Locos. Flaco was the middle son, he served as the right-hand man to the gang leader Gordo. Flaco would also start an offshoot of the gang called La Familia which would act as an umbrella for just about every gang that was a rival of Sur 13 and the West Side Locos. Sapo was the youngest, and true to form, he was the most violent and felt like he had the most to prove.

Mariana and the family lived at 1211 4th Avenue East in Bradenton, FL. In addition to the three boys, there were three daughters and dad lived in the house too. Needless to say it was a packed house but the kids never went without food, clothing, water, power, or anything else that they needed. As the BPL were being formed and gaining a reputation for being a violent criminal street gang, Mariana would deny that the gang even existed, just as many other naïve moms have done for years. The difference here was that Mariana wasn't naïve to what was going on. Mariana used her words and actions on law enforcement in an effort to keep us off of their trail. Mariana would often times cook dinner for Pieper and Ski and she would always invite them into the residence for whatever they needed. Mariana would continually argue that her kids weren't in a gang but that Sur 13 gang members were always picking on them. Mariana even gave Pieper a CD that had several Sur 13 gang members, to include Hugo and Carlos, rapping on it talking about killing Mariana and her kids. There were so many drive-by shootings at their house that the other neighbors would conduct "drive-by" drills just as many

Figure 9.1 A "War Wall."

families in the Midwest will conduct tornado drills. Believe me when I say that having those families come in and tell those stories about the "drive-by drills" and not being able to BBQ were extremely moving for the jury to hear when Pieper did a R.I.C.O. on the BPL.

As the years went on, 1211 4th Avenue East became a safe house for gang members and many young girls that would run away from home to hideout at. In the beginning Mariana would turnover whoever Pieper and Ski were looking for except for her kids. At some point Mariana got tired of Pieper and Ski always knocking on her door and taking kids away. Many of the girls would end up working for Mariana at the maid service that she ran. According to many of the girls that were working for Mariana she would take their check and hold it for an extended period of time and then tax them severely when she would finally pay them. I guess it was a small price to pay for them to stay at her house, drink, smoke, and hang out with gang members. Mariana got so bold that she began to sign fellow gang members out of the juvenile jail acting as their parents. Several mothers of the kids that she was signing out became very irate and decided to press charges on her for interfering with child custody. When Mariana was on the stand she was even wearing the gang's colors which Pieper was quick to point out to the judge. Mariana's gang name was El Black Widow, and to this day she is revered as a mentor and a role model for younger children. Mariana ended up serving almost a year in county jail for her actions and Mr. Sancho is now in prison for a third time doing a 10-year bid for R.I.C.O, Flaco is serving 15 years for R.I.C.O., and Sapo is serving 25 for an armed home invasion.

In these three examples, we have talked about three different types of mothers, one who desperately wanted to keep her kid away from the gang, one who protected her kids from the police, and another that took an active role in the gang's activities. None of these kids have managed to stay out of the gangster lifestyle or prison. That is how strong the appeal is of the gang. It provides its members with all the ingredients to make a hardened criminal through the glamorizing of money, cars, sex, girls, booze, and violence (Figure 9.1).

10 When Efforts Fail

When linking the theoretical framework to this book, the approach we have taken is the socio-cultural approach. It is based on Vygotsky's idea of social-learning and development which describes how individuals learn from their society and how the society influences learning development. According to Vygotsky's theory, younger gang members learn from previous generations of gangs and influence their practices. Parenting plays a critical role in the development of children. "Early discipline failures are a primary causal factor in the development of conduct problems. Harsh discipline, low supervision, lack of parental involvement all add to the development of aggressive children" (Dr. Gerald Patterson). Youth join gangs because of drugs, boredom, outside influences, social problems, and denial. The juvenile mindset is that it's better being in a gang then out because it's like going to college; there's activities, training, etc. In reviewing the totality of the circumstances herein, robust and sustainable efforts must identify the root causes.

In Manatee County, Florida, there was a social worker who was extremely goodhearted and wanted nothing but to help the community and children. She was well known to the Manatee County Sheriff's Office and several other agencies in that area. Towards the latter half of the first decade of the new millennium, she had come to several different groups and discussed starting a talk group for gang members who wanted to get out of the gangs that they were in. Originally, when people heard the idea they thought it was going to be an excellent social program for the community. And in truth the idea within itself was an excellent one. However, some things that are thought up on the drawing board need much more attention to detail than others. While this persons intentions were exemplary, the way in which the program ultimately worked was less than what the outcome was hoped to be.

Both Plonczynski and Pieper were two of many people that were originally consulted prior to the program being started. Both Bradenton Police Department's Gang Unit and the Manatee County Sheriff's Office Gang Unit were in full support of the idea of having gang members get out of their perspective gangs, however the way in which this program was set up had many details that still needed to be ironed out. The program was relatively simple and was based on the premise that several gang members from different groups would come to one location and speak in a group about getting out of the gang. The list of problems with starting such a program, however, were numerous. The idea of several gang members coming together in one location even if they were prior gang members caused safety concerns. Moreover, the fact and knowledge that this meeting would be in existence on a regular basis could potentially cause current and disgruntled gang members to want to come to this location to do violence to members of their own gang who are currently wanting to get out or to potential rivals and thusly would have been in need of great security. To Garrick Plonczynski, getting out of the gang was no different than giving up alcohol. When an alcoholic finally sees that the alcohol has taken over his life and there is nothing else, then and only then will they make the true, conscious decision to get clean. The same can be said with narcotics. When a drug user sometimes sees that the narcotics have taken over their lives and nothing remains of who they were except for the high and wanting to get high, then and only then will they really see the need to come clean. And just like alcohol or narcotics, getting out of the gang and getting clean from the gang is never easy. The path from a gang member in good standing with the gang to that of a former gang member that's totally clean is a very difficult journey. Very few gang members will seek out help in order to get out of the gang. Seeking help from an outside group or source is a foreign concept to most gang members. People who join gangs quickly learn to turn to the gang for everything that they need, whether it be a feeling of camaraderie, a feeling of social acceptance, a need for things such as money through narcotics sales, or whatever the case might be. After such a long time in the gang it becomes a foreign idea to go outside of the gang for anything that's needed in the way of help. As such, this idea of a social program whereby gang members would go to talk about getting out was going to have a rough start. The program did start however, and took place at the Manatee County Sheriff's Office and it was decided that tactical Gang Unit officers would be present during these meetings off to the side strictly as a security precaution. The idea of having such a program at the Sheriff's Office no doubt weighed heavily on both children and adults looking to get out of the gang as a questionable place to have this type of meeting. Moreover, to have the very people who may have arrested you in the past in the very same room where you're talking about your issues trying to get out of the gang with other people could be very intimidating. At first the program did have attendance. There was never a packed room and there never would be. During some weeks it was only one or two people that would show up, as was more often than not. However, the program did go on and as it went forward it experienced several hiccups. It's important to ask oneself these questions when thinking about such a program and implementing one. If you were a gang member, would you want to go to the Sheriff's Office for an hour or longer once a week? Would you want to be in the same room as the people that you saw out in the street repeatedly either arresting you or your friends? If the system has done nothing but harass you in the past why would you want to go to a building that represents the system to have the meeting to get out of the gang? In truth security concerns overrode all questions. It had to be that way.

Along the way a certain individual who is in the criminal street gang Sur 13 found out about this meeting. He had known the social worker for a long time and had worked with her in the past. This gang member truly believed that sooner or later he was going to be arrested on a racketeering charge. As a result he started going to these meetings without having any kind of want or desire to get out of the gang. Rather the only reason he was going into these meetings was because he knew for a fact that should he ever be arrested and his gang membership came into question, either at sentencing or as a result of the actual charge, he now had a defense. This was originally one of the problems that both Pieper and Plonczynski had spoken to each other about prior to the first meeting and as such law enforcement had known that something like this would have happened sooner or later. This gang member had actually been present to a gang murder and as such was a very dangerous person to have in the room. This gang member had no intention of getting out of the gang. He had actually been there to obtain information about rival gangs and give the appearance that he was fully committed to getting out. When he was arrested again he would be able to use this class in court to show that he was no longer in the gang. It was shortly later that Plonczynski had put together charges for racketeering to include this individual. Originally when the defense was made this gang member brought up the fact that he had been going to these meetings and in fact had been trying to get out of the gang. The defense was quashed simply by showing that this gang member was still hanging out with gang members during the time that he was going to these meetings.

Even as such, the meetings still took place and to the credit of the social worker who was the only one person to have faith and belief in the idea, and who took the time to speak with these kids, eventually the courts started using these meetings as part of a rehabilitation program for troubled kids who committed crimes and were in gangs. This was the beginning of the end. Once the court started forcing children to attend a program that had not originally been intended for that reason, the program in itself was doomed. Forcing children that had committed crimes who did not want to get out of the gang to go to a meeting whereby they were going to be expected to talk about getting out of the gang was never what this idea had originally been intended for and as a result this type of program was ill-equipped to handle these additional juveniles that were court mandated to go to these meetings as a part of their probation.

It was several months after the court had originally started mandating meeting attendance as part of the juvenile's probation that the meetings were canceled. The social worker never found a long-term partner or a second person to help them with these meetings, or who was in support of these meetings. Taking out a program of this magnitude is much bigger than one person could handle. The social worker had taken a very large problem and did her very best to put a Band-Aid on it. The program actually may have helped several of the juveniles who attended in various different ways, but there will never be any kind of follow-up study to determine what the outcomes were of these juveniles who did attend the program prior to the court starting to mandate these meetings as a part of probation. Getting back to getting out of the gang, and how it is similar to that of a person wishing to get clean from drugs or narcotics, the second that someone stepped into that room and was forced to stay there for a reason other than

Figure 10.1 A Warning of What Happens to Sur 13 "Ratas" Who Snitch to the Police.

wanting to be there, the program was set on auto destruct. By having these children in the meetings that did not want to get out of the gang, the program was allowing a cancer to manifest within itself with all of the negative attitudes that were brought into these types of meetings by gang members who did not want to get out of the gang. Plonczynski and Pieper both spoke to several of the juveniles after the meetings had been ceased and the program had been terminated. Several juveniles thought it was a great idea, but when they attended they were not 100% sure that they wanted to get out of the gang. They hadn't reached that rock-bottom point in their lives where they knew that this had to happen. As such in some cases, they continued their criminal lives and it wasn't until later that they were finally able to either move away or step back from the gang. If this program or any other program such as this is ever going to succeed, it would need more support and understanding from both the community and several other agencies (Figure 10.1).

11 Suppression

The new normal, in law enforcement, has to respond to gang problems across the country. Youth gangs and gang activity have been reported in almost all 50 states by law enforcement and media reports (Spergel et al., 1990). Major cities to rural areas that have manpower, monies, and bureaucratics buy in, have implemented gang intervention strategies, community policing, and suppression units to address gangs in their areas. These gang programs, although their effectiveness is limited by tight budgets and understaffing (Jackson & McBride, 1996; Spergel, 1995), are still utilized in many law enforcement agencies across the country. The problem is that when law enforcement puts pressure on gangs in their community, they push the problem out to the neighboring communities. Those communities may not have the resources to handle the problem as they may have never seen gangs. Another issue is the growth of transnational gangs and that has been a dangerous side effect of our failure to control the U.S.-Mexico border. As long as the United States is not unified on efforts, gangs will win.

Gangs are a global issue and no longer only in major metropolitan areas. Midsized and even small rural towns are reported to serve as hosts to the growing problem of youth gangs (Barber, 1993; Beyer, 1994; Klein, 1995; Quinn & Downs, 1993; Spergel et al., 1990; Zevitz & Takata, 1992). The shift of youth gangs from large cities to midsized or small cities is a result of displaced urban populations, high unemployment, and other social problems such as poverty and social isolation (Owens and Wells, 1993; Spergel et al., 1990). Most of the research that has addressed youth gangs in midsized or small cities has been based on the social conditions or gang indicators used in large cities (Klein, 1995; Maxson, Klein, & Gordon, 1987; Rosenbaum & Grant, 1983). In addition, research also suggests that such indicators may not always be applicable to smaller cities (Beyer, 1994; Huff, 1990; Tindle, 1996). Suppression is advised when all other aspects in the three-phase cycle of prevention, intervention, and suppression fail.

Suppression will never solve the gang issue but may in some instances be the only way to take the fight to gangs. There are varying levels of suppression that cover the gamete of scenarios according to age group (youth to adult scenarios). Depending on the deviant behavior, there are varying prosecutorial means to include enhancements that can be enacted. One of the key concepts is to quarantine the gangs and ensure they do not move their enterprises to another jurisdiction. Kicking the can down the road does not bode well for anyone and it's paramount that all jurisdictions do everything they can to take the gang threat off their streets. There are street injunctions at their disposal.

Brzenchek is enrolled in the same PhD program—Public Service Leadership and Criminal Justice at Capella University with Lauren Laielli. Detective Laielli was approached to augment discussion in this book because of her in-depth practitioner and educational perspectives. She is currently a detective in the State of New Jersey with 7 years of law enforcement experience. Over the course of her career, Detective Laielli has investigated juvenile gangs, street gangs, outlaw motorcycle gangs, and white supremacy extremist gangs. Detective Laielli holds a B.A. in Communications and Criminal Justice and an M.A. in Criminal Justice and Forensic Psychology.

Juvenile Gangs

Juvenile gangs are unique in the spectrum of gang investigation and suppression. I have found the majority of juvenile gangs tend to take accreditation as a set of a larger adult street gang, such as the Bloods or the Crips. In addition, juvenile street gangs are almost always formed in and named after a section of town in which these juveniles reside. I have interviewed many juvenile gang members during the course of my career. During the course of any interview with a member of a gang, I always inquire as to the individual's reason for joining the gang. When it comes to juveniles, I have heard many motives; however a few explanations were the most consistent answers: (a) an unstable home life, to include a lack of a parental figure or discipline; (b) the gang provided desirable items or services to these juveniles, such as money, safety, a feeling of family, and notoriety amongst peers; and (c) the juvenile "had to" due to the location of where the juvenile resided (Figure 11.1).

The findings from my personal experiences lend support to Thornberry and colleagues' path model of the origins of gang membership (Thornberry, Krohn, et al., 2003; Thornberry, Lizotte, et al., 2003). These scholars proposed that neighborhood-level and family-structure variables have a strong influence in juveniles' risks to join a gang. Essentially, this model suggests that as conventional bonds, such as familial or school bonds, weaken, the risk for the elevation of delinquency and acceptance of anti-social behaviors increases. It is theorized that these weakened bonds, internalization of anti-social values, and delinquent behaviors lead the juvenile to become attracted to the perceived benefits of joining a gang (Thornberry, Krohn, et al., 2003; Thornberry, Lizotte, et al., 2003).

When looking at suppression techniques for juvenile gangs, there needs to be a multi-faceted approach. As research and my personal experience has found, juveniles join gangs primarily due to the lack of a stable family structure, parental oversight, and peer influences, which lead to the acceptance or internalization of anti-social values. Therefore, juvenile gang suppression efforts must concentrate on strengthening the quality of juveniles' home, school, and social bonds.

Figure 11.1 Gang Graffiti on a House in a Gang-Infested Neighborhood.

WSE Gangs

During the most recent years of my career, I have focused on investigating white supremacy gangs and white supremacy extremists. White supremacy gangs are difficult to categorize, track, and number as there are a large number of these gangs, with new gangs consistently forming. These gangs tend to be loosely organized and/or closely associated with outlaw motorcycle gangs. Yet they hold various belief systems, goals, and objectives. In most recent years, I have dealt primarily with the State Prison Skinheads, the Atlantic City Skinheads, The Hammerskins, the Aryan Brotherhood, and various other small sets of white supremacy gangs. These gangs, and countless other white supremacy gangs, are considered to be not only hate groups, but domestic terrorists. This categorization of these gang members as terrorists makes the investigation and suppression unique (Figure 11.2).

In addition to typical illegal acts committed by mainstream street gangs, such as narcotics and weapons trafficking, acts of violence against rival gangs, and money laundering, these gangs add an additional component, which is the element of hatred. Historically, and in the present day, members of these gangs will commit hate crimes against minorities in the furtherance of their movement or cause. In addition, these hate crimes are viewed by these gangs as way to gain notoriety, and thus increase membership.

Figure 11.2 White Supremacist.

The key to the suppression of these gangs appears to be the removal of the leader of the gang. This can be achieved via imprisonment of the leader or separation of the leader, if the gang is in prison. For example, the Atlantic City Skinheads (ACS) were one of the more organized white supremacy gangs. ACS had a strong presence in the Atlantic City area and were well known. However, in 2005, one of the more prominent members was arrested and sentenced to life in prison for the murder of a black female in Atlantic City. In addition, in 2011, their "leader" was struck and killed by lightning. These two significant losses to the organizational structure has made ACS almost obsolete. Obviously, the goal of imprisoning a gang leader would ideally occur prior to any hate crimes being committed, which is why it is important for law enforcement to observe these gangs for signs of any illegal activity.

In February of 2006, Pieper and his partner at the time had created the Braden-ton Police Departments Gang Unit and had been busting their butts identifying as many gang members as they could. It was around this time they had learned that Sur 13 is hands down the biggest and baddest gang with well over 600 doc-umented members and associates in the city of Bradenton and Manatee County. The gang's criminal activity had included criminal mischief (gang graffiti on just about every fence and wall in the city), nightly drive-by shootings, firebombing cars, and drug dealings. The gangs did all these crimes but were most notorious for using heavy weapons in shootings. Pieper and his partner had been working with Plonczynski, (or just Ski for short) and Ski's partner for the last several months and had what they believed was a good understanding of who all the players were and where they resided and/or hung out.

One brisk night while Pieper and his partner were patrolling the known gang "hot spots" they observed two Hispanic males walking westbound on 10th Ave E. This territory was known to be turf of the East Side Crips (Figure 11.3).

This was evident by the "tagging" that was on every stop sign, industrial build-ing, abandoned, and sometimes not abandoned, house from 1st St. East to 9th St East, 9th Ave East to 13th Ave East. At that time there was about twelve houses that were occupied by members of the East Side Crips with about 20 members residing in them. At about 1:30 in the morning, Pieper saw two subjects that were walking in the middle of the road which is considered a traffic violation

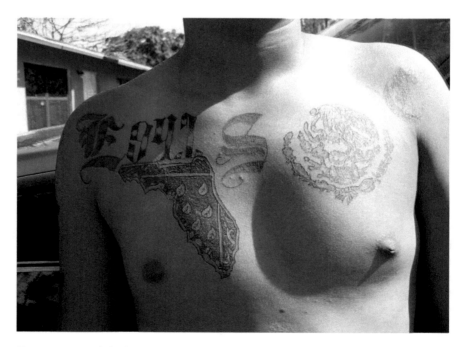

Figure 11.3 East Side Crip Tattoo.

under Florida State Statute. Pieper pulled up next to the subjects and asked them to stop. Both subjects stop as directed. Pieper made contact with Carlos of the 17th Street Surenos who was wearing a dark blue shirt, black Dickie pants, blue Nike Cortez shoes with white laces, and a blue bandanna hanging out of his back right pocket. The bandanna had white squares around its border. This detail of the bandana's design was important as it differentiates it from the gang's rival East Side Crips. The East Side Crips used a bandanna that is also blue, worn on the same side but has "tear drops" around the border. This detail may appear small and insignificant to many, including regular patrolman, but in the Gang Unit, it was paying attention to small details that **sometimes** got you farthest in the investigation.

12 Final Contact

Hugo

In January 2009, Pieper responded to the residence of one of Sur 13's female members. While *en route*, dispatch advised that she had stated that Hugo and several other Sur 13 gang members had just shot at her, the family's residence, and her brother. The victim stated that Hugo had pulled up in a smaller red car and was the front seat passenger. The victim stated that she and her brother had words with Hugo and then he suddenly began to shoot at them. There appeared to be no rhyme or reason for the altercation as both she and Hugo were Sur 13 members. The victim stated that she believed that Rodrigo, who was Sur 13 but of a different clique, was the driver and that Pedro A. of Sur 13 (in Hugo's 17th St clique) was also in the vehicle. It was a well-known fact that Pedro lived just around the corner from the shooting location. So the clear thing to do for Pieper was to go to Pedro's house. Hugo was always known to hide at Pedro's whenever he was on the run and needed a place to crash. Pieper pulled around the corner and saw the suspected vehicle pull out of Pedro's house. He gunned the car's engine and activated his emergency lights to stop the vehicle. He quickly notified dispatch of his activity and location and called for back-up officers to respond. Upon making contact with the vehicle, he quickly noticed that Rodrigo was the driver and another of Sur 13s members in the IBS clique was also in the vehicle. Pieper had actually just dropped two warrants off to the court clerk the previous day on the passenger and as soon as backup had arrived, quickly and carefully placed him under arrest. Rodrigo was detained for further questioning in regards to the shooting and Pieper then returned to Pedro's house to talk to his mother, who was a complete trainwreck. Pedro's mother came to the door and without Pieper even asking a single question or uttering a single word, she said "He's in the shower." Pieper asked who was in the shower. Pedro's mother stated that Hugo had just gotten home and was taking a shower. This was great news. Here was the suspect's car leaving this house with one of the persons identified by the victim as having been involved in the shooting. Pieper had the shooter at the house where the suspect's car was observed leaving just a short time earlier and now was Hugo, who was identified as the shooter, having just gotten home, presumably in the same suspect vehicle that the victim identified. Pieper and his back-up officers quickly made their way to the bathroom where it was clear that someone was in fact taking a shower. Pieper shouted several commands for Hugo to come out of the shower and after a few moments, Hugo did and Pieper once again was placing Hugo in handcuffs for yet another shooting charge. Just as in the past Hugo refused to talk and later charges were dropped.

Javier

May 21, 2007 was a Monday night. At approximately 8:15 that evening on the 3300 block of 5th St., East in Bradenton, Florida a fight between two rival gangs began. Members of the East Side Crips and members of Sur 13 had somehow met at this location and began to have a verbal argument. As they did so, a large crowd formed. Members from the surrounding community including apartments and homes came to see what all of the trouble was about. In this part of town, it's very common to have many people out on the street this time of night. Some witnesses stated that the verbal threats escalated to a physical fight. Other witnesses stated that there were never any fists flying, just bullets. In most likelihood both sides had guns, however it was the Suenos that had pulled guns first. On this day, Javier had been with two other males and one female in a white convertible vehicle. As the fight escalated, Javier pulled a firearm and shot 4 to 6 times. It's possible that the vehicle was moving as he shot and therefore his aim was not that accurate, not that anyone's accuracy is all that good when it's coming from a moving vehicle. As the vehicle that Javier was in started to leave the area at an extremely high rate of speed, Javier was observed standing up in the back of the convertible vehicle firing his handgun. It was at this time that one of the rounds struck a 9-year-old child. That 9-year-old child was not a gang member, was not a gang associate, but nothing more than an innocent bystander and collateral damage to the gang shooting (Figure 12.1).

Law enforcement was quickly called and responded to the scene. The 9-year-old victim was rushed to the area hospital by his father and his father's friend, however the child passed away prior to getting any sufficient life saving techniques at the hospital.

As first responders arrived at the scene, they quickly obtained the information needed in determining what occurred and who the suspects were. Immediately upon speaking to area residents, investigators learned that a gang fight had occurred. It was during the course of the initial interviews with area witnesses to the gang fight that the name Javier was first learned as one of the suspect vehicle occupants and as the shooter himself. A B.O.L.O. was immediately issued for information on Javier.

Detective Plonczynski was off duty that day. He been home alone just watching TV when he received a call from another deputy. This deputy advised Ski that there had been a shooting and the name Javier had been obtained as the name of a possible shooter. This deputy then asked Ski if he knew of any gang members with that name who possibly had a white convertible vehicle.

Figure 12.1 Bradenton Gang Member.

Plonczynski stated that he had only known of one such subject and that this person was a member of the criminal street gang Sur 13. Plonczynski went on to tell the deputy that he had been informed that Javier of Sur 13 had been observed driving such a vehicle. Detective Ski was told that the victim of the shooting was a juvenile and that it appeared that juvenile had died. Plonczynski explained to the deputy that he needed to make contact with a supervisor, however he was coming in to aid in the investigation even though he was off duty. Pieper was immediately contacted by Ski. Plonczynski relayed all of the information that he had obtained so far and requested that Pieper and his Gang Unit respond to Javier's residence and immediately set up a surveillance (as it was in Pieper's jurisdiction). Ski then contacted a friend and who was an agent in the Florida Department of Law Enforcement, and requested additional help from him and his unit. After doing so, Ski contacted Pieper once again and explained that he needed to know if Javier was home or if it appeared as if Javier was home. Ski responded to the shooting location in East Bradenton. He met deputies on scene and spoke briefly to them in an attempt to determine whether they had fresh information. He then went to the detective that was on scene and spoke to him about the facts that this detective had up to this point. Ski learned no new information but explained that the Bradenton Police Department was already conducting surveillance on a possible suspect's house.

After meeting quickly with other law enforcement, Detective Ski met with a good friend and local agent from the Florida Department of Law Enforcement. Together they began to head to the location where Pieper was conducting his surveillance. While en route, Pieper called Plonczynski and stated that the parents of one of the gang members that may have been involved (the only female in the suspect's car) had contacted him. These parents were requesting to meet at an area 7 Eleven and speak to investigators. As Pieper wasn't able to leave the surveillance, and no other units were available to conduct this interview, Plonczynski along with his counterpart from the Florida Department of Law Enforcement responded to meet the parents. Both made the best speed possible in getting there, knowing full well that area law enforcement wasn't giving out tickets. You see, so many units were tied up on the homicide from all agencies that the only remaining units that were not on this call were breaking their back going from call to call that were still going out for service. Those cops were earning their pay (as all do, when a call such as this one goes out). Upon arriving at the 7 Eleven Plonczynski immediately recognized the parents. One of the parents was a well-known West Side Loco that Plonczynski had numerous encounters with previously (most of them good). The first thing that these parents stated to investigators was that they had been told that Javier had shot someone. While speaking to the parents, Plonczynski learned that their white Chrysler Sebring convertible had been taken earlier in the evening by their daughter and her boyfriend Sleepy. The whereabouts of their daughter were unknown as were the whereabouts of her boyfriend Sleepy. While speaking to the parents, Plonczynski learned that Sleepy was also one of the suspects believed to be in the car during the shooting. To Plonczynski's surprise, he was told that the parents had already gone to Javier's home much earlier in the evening and found their white Sebring convertible parked along the curb in front of the house where Javier resided. While they were there they observed Sleepy next to the car. They asked him where their daughter was and had been told that she elected to walk home. Plonczynski then made contact with Pieper to get an update and learned that there was a lot of traffic, both coming to and leaving the house. Plonczynski asked if he believed that this was common to have this many people coming to and from this house on a weeknight. Pieper advised that it most likely was not. As this interview progressed, Plonczynski who was a gang detective, requested a homicide investigator to come and speak to these parents. One later arrived and explained that a photo pack line up had been conducted with one of the witnesses. They had identified Javier as the shooter. Plonczynski was told by the Homicide Detective that he would continue the interview of the parents. Plonczynski, along with several members of the Violent Crimes Task Force, the Florida Department of Law Enforcement, and Manatee County Sheriff's Office Criminal Investigations Division then went to the location where Pieper was conducting his surveillance.

Upon Plonczynski's arrival, all units that were conducting surveillance and that had come along with him to Javier's home moved in. What was immediately noticeable upon surrounding the home was the fact that the white Sebring convertible was still parked outside next to the curb in front of the house (Figure 12.2).

Figure 12.2 Vehicle Used in the Murder.

Plonczynski put his hand on the hood to see if the vehicle had been moved recently, however, the hood was cold and it was quite evident that the vehicle hadn't been moved for a little while. Plonczynski's sergeant at the time first made contact with Javier's mom. She had come outside to see why all the law enforcement were in her yard area this late at night upon hearing noises outside of her house. The supervisor quickly explained the circumstances surrounding what had occurred and asked her for permission to speak to Javier. Javier's mother began crying and agreed to the interview. She then stated that Javier and his brother, who was also a Sur 13 member, had been home and had been receiving friends for some time. Seconds later, as law enforcement was permitted to go inside the home and get Javier, he exited the front door. Plonczynski, who was closest to the door, went to grab him believing that Javier would possibly take off on foot if given the opportunity. As Plonczynski raised his hands to grab Javier, Javier shouted for Plonczynski to get his fucking hands off of him. Plonczynski, having another idea in mind, grabbed Javier by the left arm and brought it behind Javier into an arm bar, where he quickly placed handcuffs on him and told him he was under arrest. Plonczynski then stood by with Javier until another unit was summoned and able to place him in the back of a marked patrol car to be taken away for further interview at the Manatee County Sheriff's Office. While still on scene, Plonczynski and Pieper were informed that a search warrant was forthcoming and to seal off the home, which they did with crime scene tape (Figure 12.3).

Figure 12.3 Javier's House Right after the Murder.

While law enforcement stood by and waited for the search warrant to arrive, a young Hispanic male and his guardian came to the location where law enforcement had set up in anticipation of receiving the search warrant. Once there this guardian explained that for some reason law enforcement was searching for this young Hispanic male. It wasn't known to this law enforcement officer, however, that this young male was Sleepy. When the juvenile was asked why law enforcement was searching for him, he only replied that he didn't know. Believing otherwise the law enforcement officer asked if this guardian would drive Sleepy to the Manatee County Sheriff's Office for an interview. The guardian stated that she would drive from there immediately.

While Pieper and Plonczynski continued to wait, they noticed a large amount of graffiti on the walls of the garage and fence. Plonczynski took photos to document that the gang activity was rampant at this location in case it was needed for court at a later time.

At approximately 2:22 in the morning, the search warrant was read to Javier's mother and brother prior to the search being conducted. Pieper and Plonczynski immediately made for Javier's room. It was numerous Deputies, Officers, and Special Agents who searched the house and it took several hours. Plonczynski's supervisor played a very supportive part in getting everyone on the same page, like a conductor to an orchestra. He knew his people's talents and due to the great work between all of the agencies (such as F.D.L.E. and Bradenton Police Department), he knew the capabilities of the others on scene as well. No one was rushed, no one wanted to miss anything. The team worked for several hours in the house going over item by item to see if there was a connection. The F.D.L.E. agents who had worked with Plonczynski earlier that night conducting interviews had chosen to search the attic of the home. This part of the search can usually be very rewarding or the biggest pain in the butt. Searching an attic midday in Florida is no fun in the summer. At nighttime it doesn't get much better. For several hours this Special Agent of F.D.L.E. was meticulous in his search. Every Christmas tree ornament and stocking that had been stored away was searched. Nothing was going to be missed. The siblings bedrooms were searched as well. However, the sibling's rooms yielded no clues. Gang paraphernalia was also listed in the search warrant and plenty of it was located and seized by investigators. Plonczynski took numerous photos both inside and outside of the house believing that the gang aspect to this crime would later weigh heavily in court (Figures 12.4 and 12.5).

Figure 12.4 Javier's Bedroom during the Search Warrant.

Figure 12.5 Backyard Where Law Enforcement Fulfilled the Search Warrant.

Investigators later followed up to determine whether Sleepy had ever been driven to the Manatee County Sheriff's Office as requested, and learned that he had not been. They later went to his house and by this time had attained probable cause for his arrest. Upon going to the home, they located him and arrested him for his part in this crime.

A day later, after speaking to various parents and obtaining permission to speak to these juveniles, Plonczynski and a homicide investigator went to the juvenile detention facility located in Manatee County and there they interviewed numerous Sur 13 members. One of these Sur 13 members had been Sleepy. Rather than question him about the homicide they questioned him as to his gang involvement. He admitted to both investigators that he had been a criminal street gang member in Sur 13, specifically the 17th St. clique. This was the same group that Javier had been a part of. While speaking to investigators he had stated that he had been jumped in approximately one year earlier and he advised these investigators that his street name was indeed Sleepy.

While these investigators were still at the juvenile detention facility they were also able to interview the female that had been in the car during the shooting. Post-Miranda she had stated that she originally had been a member of the "Overpass Gang," often referred to as O.P.G. She told investigators that she used to date a different Sureno, however she now dated Sleepy. When she was asked how it was allowed that she could date a male from a rival gang, she admitted to investigators that she was no longer with O.P.G. but now represented Sur 13. Plonczynski had felt like he had just taken the weight of the world off of his shoulders. If this case was to go to trial, trying to explain how rival gang members were in the same car might have posed a difficulty to the prosecution. With this statement investigators no longer needed to explain gang culture to the jury. In the following days and weeks of this heinous crime, there was a great news coverage and media reporting on the subject. The state attorney's office for Manatee County placed one of its most competent and brightest prosecutors in charge of this case. Originally, the three suspects had been charged by investigators with discharging a firearm from a vehicle. This is a felony in the state of Florida, however as probable cause did not exist at that time to prove that the murder was a direct result from Javier firing his gun from the convertible, they were only charged with a lesser crime. On June 1, the state attorney's office took the action against all three defendants and changed their criminal charges from discharging a firearm from a vehicle to murder in the 2nd degree. The state also elected to file on all three juveniles as adults.

The days then turned to weeks and the weeks to months. The homicide consumed a lot of time for both Pieper and Plonczynski. Jail mail was monitored, as were visitations and phone calls for all three suspects. When you start to follow up on an investigation such as a murder of this magnitude, it sooner or later consumes you. This homicide investigation would yield three more arrests and later be used as a predicate act in a racketeering charge against several of the members of Sur 13. It was to be the communities' most heinous crime of the year, and for several years to come would weigh heavily on both Pieper and Plonczynski.

Sniper

October 2, 2006, there was a stabbing in a neighboring county. Numerous people were stabbed in a fight with over 50 people involved. It occurred at one of the most popular nightclubs in Sarasota called Club Pure. Both Pieper and Plonczynski had drank there more times than anyone could count. Pieper had worked there as a bouncer before he had been a cop. The stabbing was gang related and the lead agency no longer had a Gang Unit. They had disbanded the one they had 2 years previously, thinking they no longer had a gang problem. Not a good call. At 2:00 am Plonczynski got a call from their lead detective needing to know about a kid. All they had was a street name, "Sniper." Both Plonczynski and his partner knew Sniper well. He was a member of Sur 13 and the brother of the gang's leader and most violent member. Plonczynski had arrested Sniper three months earlier for possessing a machine gun (no joke, it was a WWII Nazi stamped MP-40), so Plonczynski had become well acquainted with him. He knew his home address, cars he drove, hangouts, and baby mommas right off the top of his head. He gave the detective what he knew. The next day Plonczynski got a call to get Sarasota's investigators pictures of Sniper, as they couldn't find any. It was his day off. So he and his son, Aaron, went to the office and they faxed what they had. Mind you this was before the management was told that anything work related had to be compensated for. More often than not, both Plonczynski and his partner worked for free and never mumbled a word about coming in during times like this. Work ethic and reputation were everything and working for free on the weekends, well it sometimes just happened. While Plonczynski and his son Aaron were walking through the halls of the Sheriff's Office, other detectives were bringing in a Norte 14 member. Plonczynski knew the gang member well and had a good rapport with him. He was in handcuffs and said hello and asked if Aaron was his son. Plonczynski didn't hide anything and stated that he was (mostly because Aaron was too young to lie and not to say something about it later. Moreover, who else could Aaron belong to, Plonczynski wasn't the damn baby sitter at the office). This would be a memorable day as Aaron had been introduced to the first gang member he would ever meet. The Sarasota detective used the pictures of Sniper Plonczynski had sent, did photo lineups, and got probable cause for the arrest. Not a bad day's work based on him and Aaron spending two hours in the office. That was the first time Aaron was with Plonczynski while he worked on a big case. It was Plonczynski's turn to have custody for the weekend so Aaron came along. It wasn't the last time that this would happen either. Later, Aaron would have real nightmares about the encounter. A gang member in handcuffs talking to your father at 4 years old is something you don't easily forget, something his mother never let Plonczynski forget.

The next day Jack, the Sarasota detective, called again. He told Plonczynski to find Sniper and arrest him based on his probable cause. Based on Florida's fellow office rule, all that law enforcement was required to do was make sure there was probable cause and deputies or officers could affect the arrest based on another law enforcement officer's articulation that there was probable cause for the arrest and what the charge was. Plonczynski did question Jack at length on how he obtained the probable cause, what facts he had, and so on. It wasn't that he didn't trust him, however his jurisdiction often thought of themselves as the world police and did stuff that he found to be a little over stepping at times.

So Plonczynski had to call his lieutenant requesting overtime to go and find Sniper. His lieutenant was an ass kicker and name taker. The lieutenant was a no nonsense woman who excelled at letting her people get what they needed to get the job done, and she told Plonczynski that he had two hours to go and find him.

It was 3:00 pm, not a time too many people can be located. At 3:00 pm where are most people on a weekday? The simple answer is work. If not there, where? Home, running errands, whatever, but it is a terrible time to hunt as any warrant office will tell you. Plonczynski and his partner checked all the known gang hangouts, and then set up surveillance on Sniper's place. They weren't there ten minutes when Nightmare came outside then went back inside. It was unbelievable luck. Plonczynski immediately called out over the radio what they were doing, said that they were going after a murder suspect and requested dispatch to send a marked car. Sniper was Sur 13, so the possibilities of his fellow gang members being there too was 50/50. Another obstacle would be if Spider, his brother, was home. Additionally, his parents were notorious for hating the Gang Unit so there was another obstacle. Plonczynski threw down the microphone and ran to the house. In the excitement of the moment however, he forgot to grab his walkie and ran off without it.

While Plonczynski took the front, his partner took the back. Plonczynski knocked a normal knock and Sniper came out. Plonczynski went to his back pocket to call out over the radio and have his partner come to the front. Of course, having forgotten the walkie he did the next best thing and shouted for his partner. Upon realizing neither of them had hand held radios, Plonczynski's partner came up front and spoke tactfully to Sniper. Meanwhile Plonczynski called the Sarasota detective. Sniper was calm as a mountain stream. He had to have known why detectives were there. He never lost his cool though and acted as if all was right with the world. He was a wolf in sheep's clothing. This is the type of situation where you have to keep your guard up. It's easy to let your guard down when the perp appears to be relaxed and calm, but so often this is where law enforcement gets hurt the worst. Henry Carr killed two detectives and a trooper in Florida because detectives didn't do what was necessary to ensure their own safety. All law enforcement are guilty of it sooner or later. Complacency kills. This was not the case here though. No one had arrested Sniper yet so Plonczynski asked Sarasota's detective if a) they were still good to go on the arrest; and b) where they wanted to meet. When dealing with another agency, there is always a delay, roadblock, or something that comes up. Moreover, second guessing initial calls is a common practice by some units. In this case, when Plonczynski called Sarasota's detectives, Sarasota asked if they could just get him to come along back with them to Sarasota for questioning and not have him arrested. Plonczynski was pissed. He had been told to arrest Sniper and told his supervisor that the reason for the overtime was to arrest a gang member who was wanted for murder. That would have been fine had the other detectives been upfront about their intentions and updated everyone as to new plans. It also probably would have worked until Nightmare's mother pulled up into the driveway. She jacked the car door open and began shouting and yelling better than most. She had a real talent for it. At that point, Plonczynski yelled to affect the arrest and told the Sarasota detective that he hoped that Sarasota had their shit straight, as it was now too late, the arrest based on the fellow officer rule had been made. It was about this time that marked backup units arrived in numbers. They had been sent after dispatchers had been unsuccessful in raising them on the radio. This would be the same radio both had forgotten to bring. Plonczynski tried to be polite to the mother but as usual she gave him the evil eye and if looks could kill, this book may have never been written. Patrol units quickly put Sniper in the car and brought him to Manatee's criminal investigation division. After a two-hour wait for Sarasota's detectives to show up, they took over and did a two-hour interview. Sniper told them everything, except what they wanted to hear. He was charged with murder and two counts of attempted and for a day off, both Plonczynski and his partner spent ten hours helping them out. This episode ended well, but could have gone 100 different ways. That's why as gang investigators it's crucial to know the gang, know its members, and know that they are capable of anything at any time. There's an old cop saying that goes, "I'll take luck over experience every time."

October 8, 2006, Plonczynski and his partner were on duty when a call came out from the road patrol. Deputies were out with 8 to 10 Surenos in a bad part of town called Oneco and the road patrol was having a hard time with them. Patrol just wanted to get them identified and the gang members weren't having it. They didn't want to be identified. These specific gang members had been arrested numerous times and now were very well versed as street lawyers. They knew and understood a little about their rights and were making it very hard for patrol to do their job effectively. Plonczynski and his partner rode out and spoke to both patrol deputies and the Surenos. In truth, once they got there, the problem was rectified. The gang bangers knew Plonczynski and his partner well and had a lukewarm relationship with them. Carlos was among this crew that was out with patrol. All the gang members were identified for patrol without even haven spoken to them. The patrol deputies were hot. They didn't like to play games and then calling for the Gang Unit, only to have the Gang Unit know who everyone was without even speaking to them, made the patrol units a little bit upset. It appeared to them like they couldn't do their jobs and needed help. Nothing was further from the truth of course. When you work gangs all day every day, you get to know your people. Patrol in no way had lost any face, but resented looking incompetent all the same. Patrol units had gotten deep as they were getting ready to take everyone to jail as John Doe. No less than 7 patrol cars were on scene. The gang members had been true to form and did not told the deputies anything. Plonczynski learned that the reason for the initial stop was that there had been a gang fight that one side chickened out of. When the one side refused to fight, they got in their car and got more people. They then drove around until they found the other crew at a stop light. They then exited their vehicle and started breaking the windows with bats; then went home to drink some 40s.

When Plonczynski and his partner had gotten there, they quickly identified the gangs as Sur 13 and Canal Road Locos. The two gangs were always at each other's throat.

As they stood around waiting to see what the primary deputy was going to do with the call, the road supervisor came up to both Plonczynski and his partner. He began congratulating them on capturing Sniper. Word had it, that he'd been one of the other stabbing suspects from the Maggy's incident and had been involved in several drive-bys in the area. The sergeant asked how the capture/arrest had gone and then asked what they had to endure to make the arrest and hear it from their own mouths. It was an odd request, so Plonczynski asked, "Why?" The sergeant then said that he had heard the story of the arrest told in squad meeting for the road patrol units, that the two of them had sat on Nightmare's house for two days straight. Never leaving their cars, not leaving to use the bathroom, not calling for relief, not going home for sleep, and had remained vigilant for the duration until two days later when they finally caught and handcuffed Sniper for attempted murder. The two quickly looked at each other and began laughing heavily. Plonczynski took a step forward, looked him straight in the eyes and told him, "Yep, it's true."

13 Case Studies

Case Study #1

Outlaw Motorcycle Story at Camp Katrina in Mississippi:
Americas Worst Natural Disaster

In 2005, Hurricane Katrina occurred. It was the eleventh named storm and fifth hurricane of the 2005 Atlantic hurricane season. It was the costliest hurricane, as well as one of the five deadliest, ever here in the states. It was about four times the destructive force of hurricane Andrew. The hurricane wasn't believed to be a threat for the most part by too many people. It was thought to be an inconvenience at most as most hurricanes are. As the hurricane sat in the Gulf, it brewed and gained strength. It had already hit land in Miami and continued into the warmer waters of the Gulf of Mexico where it continued to gain steam. There it sat taking aim at Louisiana, Mississippi, and Alabama. When it did strike, it did so on such a grand scale that it would be called the Greatest Natural Disaster in American History. Many remember the hurricane flooding New Orleans the worst. Many other areas were flooded as well but most of the media concentrated on images of the "Big Easy." The television images were unbelievable. There was a detective that Pieper and Plonczynski worked with, that will be referred to as "Dutch," who went to the Superdome for protection. He had been there on subpoena for court and was caught between needing to stay for court and getting the hell out of town. He stayed. His story of how he was rescued and what took place to get him to safety out of the superdome is another story though and destined to be a book itself someday. After Katrina hit, conditions in the superdome became horrendous. Man became animal and Dutch had destroyed his credentials amongst other things to avoid being stopped and shot as a cop by the armed gangs that were running the superdome. Yes, that's right, gangs ran the superdome. In the absence of law, anarchy will always rule. Here was a prime example. Gang members were really shooting at the military from the Superdome and Sheriff Wells put together a team of mostly SWAT to go to the superdome, find Dutch, and bring him back home. The plan was put together rather quickly. Many people thought that more logistics needed to be done, before sending the team. The plan was very simple. Simply put, it was to put together the best shooters and biggest guys in the agency and send them, to bring Dutch home. In the end, the Texas Rangers located Dutch first and got him out alive. Rumor has it, a large team of well-trained Texas Rangers had mounted up and gone in. Dutch's cell phone was near death as there was no way to recharge it without power in the superdome. The Rangers, however, located Dutch and took him down at gun point. During the handcuffing and removal, they were surrounded by pissed off civilians asking why they had come to just get him. The Rangers told everyone that Dutch was a well-known murderer. They had no problem letting the Rangers take him then. Dutch was then delivered to the SWAT team that had been sent to get him. A great story for another time.

Within two weeks of the hurricane making landfall in the states, Plonczynski was sent to Mississippi, not as a gang investigator but rather as a disaster responder. He had been trained as such and looked forward to helping. Little did he know the hell he was walking in to.

On September 7, 2005, he was sent to Stintson airport. The first wave of responders left one week earlier so his arrival should have been easy. The second wave never has the problems of the first group. Initially the trip up was easy. He had packed everything he could into a marked car and had a mechanic with his department along with him on the trip. With all their gear, the car was packed full. They started hitting heavy gridlock traffic on the way past Crestview, Florida. Hours' worth of it. They took the "emergency lane" which was actually the side of the road. With blue lights and siren blaring they by-passed the bumper to bumper traffic. An unmarked New Orleans cop jumped into the convoy of twenty vehicles and as they slowed he pulled next to Plonczynski, flashed his police ID and credentials, and then explained who he was. He'd been on vacation when the storm hit. He wasn't due back from vacation for another week but he couldn't sit and do nothing in another state while his co-workers did the lion's share of the work. Plonczynski told him to stay in line with his agency and they would cut the path as long as they could for him. He was grateful and stayed with them until Exit 13 where they got off I-10. No one knew at the time the hell they were about to walk in to, but that was nothing in comparison to the hell he was facing. When Plonczynski pulled into the airport, he met the first wave of disaster responders, from his agency. They had nothing but horror stories. When they got there, the military was twenty-four hours behind. Deputies set up on the airport tarmac only to be kicked out by the Marines when they arrived. The military didn't care or understand that they were there to help, as well. The deputies moved to the Votech next door. They set up in one of the buildings next to the car shop. After they were all set up in their new spot, the Emergency Operations Center staff kicked them out and they had to take the garage of the Votech instead. The first group brought the sheriff's food trailer. This is a 53-foot trailer full of food and a military kitchen. They also brought an additional trailer with hundreds of gallons of gas. When the military arrived and saw what the first team had brought, the military confronted the first team, stating they were commandeering all of it. The military had been sent, but had not brought enough rations, equipment, or other items with them. The trucks they had were running out of fuel. The rations the military had brought were running low and they had no idea when they were going to be resupplied. It was a clusterfuck of the first order. A confrontation soon arose. The first responders were told by the military commander that they needed to put everything in order and would turn it all over to the military. To prevent the military seizure, the guys from the first team of responders parked their cars around the trailer and military kitchen. When the military came to take it, they were told on not so friendly terms that while the military's guns had no bullets, the deputies did and the seizure would be considered looting and met with extreme prejudice. The military commander backed down after some deliberation and serious re-evaluating. He then got on a helicopter and left. During the night though, someone came into the compound and siphoned off 85% of the gas from a 500-gallon container the that had also been brought. To this day no one knows how it was done. To take that much fuel from the container, inside the Law Enforcement compound was a feat that someone should be proud of. During Plonczynski's first day there on scene, he had a buddy show him around and being they were of the same type of breed (believing it's not what you know but who you know) introduced him to the movers and shakers in the area. Plonczynski was first brought to the main distribution center behind the law enforcement staging area. Paul and Amy were two civilians overseeing the center. The building was theirs and they had managed to start putting small things together for the community. Within one week they had the largest distribution center in the county and maybe the state. They fed the supplies to all the other sites. Plonczynski met them and was told about everything the first group had done for them. Looting was the main concern and they were very much pro-law enforcement. They believed that if they treated the first responders well, they would be treated accordingly (and they were). If they needed medical help, EMS had been on scene and would treat them immediately. They had lost their home like everyone else but had purpose in helping others. Brett Farve's (the QB at the time for Greenbay) wife had come by earlier that week with trailers of supplies and donated the stuff leaving it there. It was an unbelievable act of human kindness. Plonczynski made sure that this family remained safe and well-fed the entire time there. They wanted for nothing.

After going back to camp he was briefed on the mission. They were to protect the E.O.C. There was nothing more to the job. Now, here was a well-trained disaster responder. He was used to helping, but providing security at a Votech seemed a monumental waste of resources to him considering they had 30 people to do the job. The military was now living on three sides of the perimeter. Like many, he had come to help. Who were they supposed to protect them from?. The E.O.C. and military had to work together but the military doesn't work with anyone in the civilian world very well in these type of situations. His first night, and one gun was stolen from the Coast Guard barracks. Now they had Marines, Coast Guard, Army, National Guard, Navy, and more there.

He was later told that after Katrina had come through, that some of the first responders of the E.O.C. were held up on the road and had everything stolen by a band of looters. E.O.C. personnel then contacted the Federal government for help and protection. A call was made and they were contacted to provide security for these people. Where were the locals? Well, not one cop had a house in the area that had been left standing. One patrol car was found in a tree. Another Sheriff's patrol cruiser was found by the first team on the side of the road, unlocked. The keys in the ignition. There was no gas left in the tank. The deputy was nowhere to be found. The local sheriff was missing at first, only later to be found and relieved of all duties due to the personal strain.

Additionally, prior to Plonczynski's team arriving, someone had run a roadblock that the local law enforcement had set up after the storm. That vehicle was fired upon by the local law enforcement and the occupants taken out of the car at gun point. The local law enforcement had no way to incarcerate them. There was no jail, no court house, and no way to detain the suspects. So roadside justice prevailing, after removing the occupants, they beat the suspects and left them for dead. Upon hearing this story, the governor appointed a Florida Sheriff who promptly moved some of his own into the area and gave the local law enforcement two weeks paid vacation. The truth is they should've been given two months paid vacation.

The first night Plonczynski and his team pulled into "hell," the previous crew was set for leaving the next morning and the area was maxed out for space. There was no spare room and no place to set his kit. That night, he half slept in a bed of a pickup while mosquitos large enough to carry small children away ate freely until the sergeant came and asked him to work from 2:00 to 7:00 am. He graciously accepted the offer. He had done so just to avoid sleeping. The bugs were too big and air too hot to sleep anyways. He pulled post with a guy we will call Roger. Roger was mentally "off." He had back water values on most everything.

The following day, September 7, Plonczynski slept until 5:00 pm and got a hot meal. He learned that during that day the military had walked through the compound taking notes of what they had stock in. The military were confronted and quickly sent on their way. Things were heated still and no one trusted anything they were told by the military. That night security was increased, however the shift had been uneventful.

The next day he awoke mid-afternoon. He had been sleeping in a diving trailer during the day. This trailer was the best place to sleep and even though the noise from the airport next door with all the helicopters and planes constantly coming and going was a pain, the one big plus was that the trailer was dark and air conditioned. Every four hours the generator needed to be fiddled with but compared to the other sleeping quarters like an old school house, well, it was heaven. On this day though he hadn't slept much. He felt "green" and exhausted. Out of the trailer after only five hours sleep he was spotted by EMS personnel from back home. Medic Smith sat him down and ran the full spectrum of tests on him. Plonczynski was already looking bad. Smith said Plonczynski needed to take it easy but in the end it was only exhaustion coupled with dehydration. He was fine except for his color. Many of the others in "the compound" as they called it weren't so lucky. A lot of the first responders had a rash and illness linked from standing water in the area. Everyone tried to avoid standing water and mud like the plague, but conditions were so bad for that due to the environment and all of the water still on the ground, law enforcement was setting up tents in mud because there was nowhere else to set up. This standing mud and water thus created some illness that produced a rash. The symptoms became numerous but the rash was always present. Many became sick, too sick to work, and were sent home early. One deputy became so sick that he had to be sent home after only being in the area a couple days. Local doctors and medical personnel had no idea how to treat this rash either and for many, if you got the rash you were avoided like the plague as well. No one knew if it was contagious or not. Morale was low. The main job was to protect resources and the E.O.C. from the military who were often caught at night sneaking into the area trying to "recon" other people's belongings. Several times they were located in restricted sleeping areas. This was an area off limits to them and in one case, one soldier was almost tazed. It was on this date that many got to take their first shower in days. A trailer had been reconfigured and made into a multi-shower facility and brought in. It was a godsend to many but with the military and every law enforcement/first responder in their area, trying to get clean was a real accomplishment. Seven shower heads for hundreds of people and now they had to guard and keep security of that as well.

During the day, as Plonczynski slept, other law enforcement would go out to do work. More animals were shot then saved by law enforcement. A reality few know to this day. A horse, for example, was found on top of a school. After three days of no food and water it was finally located. When asked what to do with it, the simple response was how are we going to get it down. There was no machinery in the area for the rescue. Shooting it and throwing it over the edge of the roof was the humane and easy call. Ammunition went real quick.

On September 9 2005, Plonczynski woke up to find tour buses in the compound giving tours of the E.O.C. to civilians. Kids playing and folks taking pictures. It was absolute insanity. One deputy nearly arrested a person from M.E.M.A. (Mississippi Emergency Management Administration) who told him he wasn't needed there. M.E.M.A. had no say on anyone being there, and as a joke every question the night crew could not answer was directed at that man in M.E.M.A. I'll call "John." If someone could not get a curfew pass and asked why, "You need to ask John in MEMA" or because "John in MEMA has made that decision" was the standard response. I'm not sure if any of it got back to him, but there were lots of pissed off people looking for John in M.E.M.A. to kick his ass. If someone was refused a night pass to their property and they asked why, they would be told because John in M.E.M.A. has made that decision and doesn't believe you need to have that privilege. It ran like that for a few days if not the entire time thereafter.

That night, like all nights, Plonczynski checked out the Distribution Centers. Lots of looting was taking place (including that by the military) and Plonczynski was asked daily by those in charge of the centers to make sure the military stayed out. He had been told by all supervisors of the centers that first responders could grab anything they wanted for themselves but if they later turned out not to want it, only give it to a family. Unfortunately, some law enforcement went overboard. Plonczynski's unit had fifteen cots stolen or borrowed and never returned the first night he was there alone. So he worked hard to at least replace some of the stolen items. As the people in charge (Kevin, Paul, Sam, and Mike) of the distribution center all heard this story they gave law enforcement the full run on whatever they wanted and said so to everyone. Plonczynski and many others felt bad about the looting and did their best to make sure what was taken by law enforcement would be of immediate use. In the end, he only took two boxes of MRE's for himself. These boxes replaced the ones he gave to Emergency Services before the first team deployed. When he arrived he was told both boxes had been used and were life savers.

On the night of September 10, Plonczynski's team actually went and did work at a new distribution center. The old distribution place was called Wal-Mart. Plonczynski moved everything to a new location. They called this new place K-Mart. There they met Mark. Mark was from New York City and had just arrived. Plonczynski showed him around and told him how to get a shower and hot food. For this alone Plonczynski was given free run. Plonczynski then went to the old place, met Mike, and brought him over to meet Mark. Hours later Plonczynski came back to the nearly empty "Wal-Mart." Mike was gone and the military now had taken over the location. They had left only a private named Armstrong to work. Plonczynski gave Armstrong a cigarette and he helped find boots and an air compressor. The boots were for the day time crew who were going out to find bodies the following morning. The air compressor...well Sgt. Smith took that (in case of a flat tire that the road cars seemed to be getting a lot of). There was still a lot of crap that had not been removed from numerous streets.

That night the night crew took a group photograph. Everyone was past exhaustion.

Boredom at night was hard to fight. Deputies got a TV hooked up to a generator that night to pass the time. Other deputies and various law enforcement would be sitting in front of the TV at the C.P. watching it. Later that night, the head of E.O.C. told the deputies passing out night time passes to restricted areas and that no curfew passes could be signed any more. Looters were found the previous night with passes Plonczynski's daytime counterparts had handed out.

After deputies were told not to issue passes, the night got interesting. There was always a car coming in asking for a pass and now without passes going out, people were getting hot. Later on, some kids rode up to the main gate. They wanted to enter the compound without ID and stated their mother lived in the area and was working in the E.O.C. No identification meant no entrance. After about five minutes the mother, who was the 2nd in command at the E.O.C., came over in the bathrobe and nothing else, complaining about law enforcement not letting the kids in. There were looters in the compound, people looting on night passes and she couldn't understand why they did not let her kids without ID in the camp. She was hotter than the daytime sun with 100% humidity. The supervisor was nowhere to be found. Plonczynski spent one hour talking to her and the kids and finally got her calmed down and stopped her yelling about filing a complaint.

About 4:00 am several pickups returned to the command post. They were F.E.M.A. personnel. The pickups had come back from K-Mart or Wal-Mart (one of the Distribution Centers) loaded with cots. This was weird and the front gate deputies asked what the cots were for. They were told for F.E.M.A. persons to use. The problem was that F.E.M.A. had already been sleeping in bedded trailers. It wasn't for sleeping on now, it was for use after Katrina. F.E.M.A. people were getting greedy and had started "appropriating" for themselves, this was the beginning. By and far, F.E.M.A. workers became some of the biggest looters of Katrina. Later, TV (CNN) covered stories on such things so it was no big secret, but at the time it made everyone feel worse and worse.

One little tidbit the public wasn't told outright was that there were cold trailers set up all over the county. These were locked except to emergency workers and jam packed full of bodies and parts. Lots of them were unidentifiable and the medical examiner had to later go through each trailer and log what was there. The body numbers were unheard of and it really brought home that this was a natural disaster like none other in the past.

On September 11 Plonczynski woke up and went to the first check-in security gate. There an old squad mate from back in Plonczynski's patrol days named "Dan" was working security alone. He told Plonczynski of a weird guy working for a British Shelter Box company who had O.M.G. 1%'ers tattoo on his neck. The early morning "daze" from having just woken up went by the wayside and he quickly shook himself straight to hear the full story. This 1%'er had walked into the E.O.C. with a humanitarian group and been given a full-access pass. This pass, mind you, gave him permission into law enforcement and military sleeping areas where guns were stored. In fact, several guns had already been reported missing by several different agencies. Upon hearing this Plonczynski got dressed, located the boss of the humanitarian group of Shelter Box. As it turned out, he was a high-ranking cop in London. Plonczynski quickly explained what had occurred and this guy went ballistic. He had allowed someone else to do the hiring which was done on the fly and without any sort of background check. Plonczynski explained the situation and stated that the E.O.C. was going to revoke his full access pass and the access of all his people. After some explanation of what an Outlaw Motorcycle Gang member was along with what a 1%'er is, the owner of the company apologized for the indiscretion and promptly fired all of the people they had just hired here in the states. This was huge, as this was about 50 people that were currently in possession of full-access passes. Law enforcement then moved quickly and went to the E.O.C. and explained that they allowed full access to secure areas of the E.O.C. and surrounding compounds to a gang member. 1%'ers are typically outlaw motorcycle gang members and had no place having full access to the E.O.C. revoked all Shelter Box full-access passes and sent a representative with deputies and other law enforcement to locate this individual. With a fresh uniform on, Plonczynski went in search of this guy and found him at the mess tent. With several of deputies surrounding him (and a table full of MPs next to them) Plonczynski tactfully asked to speak to him. This guy was off his rocker from the start. His eyes were wide open and dilated to the size of half dollars. His clothing was a mess (but that was common there). He stunk of not having showered in days, although it may have been weeks. His hair was all over the place and even sticking up in several places. He stared at Plonczynski, looking him right in the eyes with a look on his face that spelled trouble. Plonczynski asked him what the 1% tattoo was about. To this date, Plonczynski had never had anyone recite such a memorized answer before. He spouted out in a loud commanding voice, the text book answer and immediately everyone standing there knew this guy was the real deal. Plonczynski explained because of his answer that he shouldn't be working in the service area. He started getting louder by yelling at deputies and making large arm movements, drawing the attention of the MPs at the next table. Plonczynski checked his six. He had put them to his back intentionally. The whole damn table was staring in this direction. Every one of the MP's looked like they were begging to get in on this and a few started to get up from the table. Plonczynski needed to make this quick. A person who exhibits this type of behavior was not rational and potentially armed, so Plonczynski then started explaining that he wasn't welcome. The E.O.C. representative issued a trespass warning and asked him to leave. As they did, the MPs came over and asked if they could help. This guy was getting louder and now really making a commotion. These guys had been itching for a fight. As things ended up though, there was no such luck. The E.O.C. revoked all of the Shelter Box employees' access passes and that night they had the responsibility of removing these people from their sleeping locations to a place outside the perimeter of the E.O.C. It was a long night and deputies worked a good portion of it, getting these people out. Most were not common folk, but homeless people and riff raff that had volunteered to help but had no business being given full E.O.C. passes to begin with.

On the 12th of September, it was the day before going home. It was a long day all in all. There would be no replacements for Plonczynski's team, so they needed to pack everything up themselves for the long trip home. They were given permission to work a 24-hour shift that morning, essentially pulling a double so they could sleep that night before they took off the next day. Unfortunately, sleeping quarters were packed away and they had no place to sleep even if they wanted to. It was a pain. Phil, a Manatee County Sheriff's Office mechanic, had been fixing cars for every department once word got out of his services. The noise from his garage alone was enough to wake the dead. National police supply had been donating police equipment including in car MDT/MDC's and installing them in the cars there as well. It was a little later that Plonczynski found out that a large group of bikers had been seen by the MPs on the perimeter. They all had "cuts" but the MPs not knowing one OMG patch from another, weren't sure what gang they were with and didn't stop any of them as it was daytime and they weren't in a restricted area. It was never determined if they were there as a result of the one OMG member that had been kicked out of the camp. That night after 24 hours of working, Plonczynski started drinking 18-year-old scotch.

Plonczynski later passed out in the garage and woke up hours later puking his guts out. He was deathly sick and EMS ended up barely pulling him back together—one cup of scotch after dehydration and a week of hell had been the final straw on the body. He remained deathly ill throughout the next day as well. On the way home, he was often observed opening the patrol car door and puking hard. It had to be a sight from the car behind him.

Case Study #2

Shooting at Scooters Bar

It was early in December 1998 when Plonczynski was working as a patrolman in the southern part of Manatee County. At approximately one o'clock on a Sunday morning in December a call went out at a local bar known as Scooters. Scooters was notoriously known to be a biker bar. There was never any calls for services at Scooters because the biker gang usually took care of their own business. Moreover, the owner was sympathetic and allowed the gang to do whatever they wanted to do while they were in the bar. On this night, someone had called 911 and said that there had been a shooting at Scooters. Plonczynski immediately told the dispatcher that he was going to be running "priority two", meaning that he was going to be traveling above the posted speed limit in emergency mode. While en route, another deputy cut them off at an intersection and Plonczynski followed him to the address of 5645 15th St., East Bradenton, Florida. This was the location of Scooters bar. Once there, both ran to the entrance way of the bar. While running inside Plonczynski was stopped by a patron and stated that they had found the wallet of the shooter out in the parking lot and this wallet was given to Plonczynski to hold. Plonczynski quickly put it in his pocket and followed the other deputy inside the bar. As Plonczynski opened the door he observed a man's face down in a pool of blood. The other deputy quickly told Plonczynski to rope off the area with crime scene tape and establish a perimeter. Other deputies soon arrived and began interviewing the patrons. Most of the patrons of the bar were members of the "motorcycle club." One of the other members of Plonczynski squad made contact with one of the gang members. The gang member was bleeding but standing and discussing things in a very calm and cool manner. EMS quickly arrived on scene and started to look at the victim on the ground as well as the subject that Plonczynski was interviewing. Plonczynski quickly started an affidavit for this victim who told him the story of what occurred. It had been a simple night with the gang in the bar shooting pool and drinking as they often did on Saturday nights there at Scooters. One of the subjects that came into the bar was not a member of the gang. He'd gotten angry over someone who allegedly stole his beer or something along those lines. This is escalated into a verbal confrontation whereby the suspect stormed to the front door and shouted that he would be back. The gang went back shooting pool, talking to women, and drinking beer and paid him no mind. It was shortly thereafter that this individual did return. The suspect then opened the door and while pointing a shotgun, made the statement "I told you I would be back mother fuckers." He then racked a round and shot point-blank at the victim with a 20-gauge shotgun. The suspect then exited Scooters to the parking lot area. One of the members of the gang that was present we will call "Big R." Big R, stood approximately 6'3" and was built like a typical NBA player. He was also the enforcer for the gang. Big R, being the enforcer, ran out the front door after the perpetrator. Encountering him in the parking lot the two began to fight. Big R was hit twice in the arm and upper torso by the shooter, as the shooter attempted to reload the firearm. During the altercation, the offender was able to locate another round, rack inside of the shotgun, and fire at the gang's enforcer. The round, being fired in haste, totally missed its target. Big R, was armed with United States Marine Corps K bar knife, which he then pulled out of the leather strapped holster and stabbed the shooter in the right cheek of his buttocks. The perpetrator then ran south into the woods and was not seen again for some time. Plonczynski interviewed the gang's enforcer for some time trying to get as much of the story straight he could. Typically this wasn't something that most outlaw motorcycle gangs would do even back in 1998. As you read this you have to remember that this is long before the days of most people having cell phones, much less smart phones or phones capable of photos and/or video. There was no video surveillance at Scooters for a very good reason. Plonczynski would later find out that the victim that had been shot below the armpit. The victim lost much of the muscle on his one arm and a bit of muscle on the side of the chest as a result of the shock him being so close when it was fired to the victim. The perpetrator would eventually end up at Manatee Memorial Hospital. When he was admitted, the Sheriff's Office was immediately notified due to the severity of the wound that had been inflicted from the enforcer's knife. The patrol deputy that responded asked only one question: where this did this occur? After the deputy had been told that the injury was obtained at Scooters bar he didn't ask any more questions, but then radioed to units on scene still at Scooters that a possible suspect had been located and was currently seeking medical treatment at Manatee Memorial Hospital. Big R had injuries that weren't life-threatening and agreed to go with law enforcement to Manatee Memorial Hospital to try and identify the person. Once there, a show up was conducted and it was confirmed that this individual with a stab wound was indeed the shooter from Scooters bar. This may have seemed like a pretty open and shut case but actually went to trial and for a short time had many involved concerned that the suspect might actually win. However, unlike most other court cases where outlaw motorcycle gang members are involved, here they were clearly the victims. During the trial that took place almost 2 years later, the courthouse was full of patched OMG club members. One would not know it to look at any of them at the time as none of them were wearing any memorabilia or paraphernalia that would indicate their membership to the gang. Plonczynski, better versed by now, knew many of them from that fateful night and realized that the people that they were associating with in the halls of the courthouse were either club associates (also known as "hang arounds") or members of the club. In the end, the offender was found guilty and subsequently sentenced to a lengthy prison sentence in the Florida Department of Corrections. It would be years later that Plonczynski would actually stop Big R, for a traffic infraction only two intersections away from where Scooters Bar was located. Scooters Bar was long gone but the gang still remained. During the traffic stop Plonczynski spoke to the enforcer. Since the time of the shooting things moved on in the gang, and this man was now the national enforcer. Plonczynski recognized him immediately during a traffic stop and called him by name. He also politely asked if Big R wouldn't mind relinquishing the giant knife on the side of his hip. Big R complied as there was no reason not to. Plonczynski quickly realized however that this man had now changed. He had nothing to say to Plonczynski, open-ended questions were not answered, and he said very little past yes or no. Plonczynski wasn't offended, wasn't angered, and he understood. This was the lifestyle and this man had gone from being the enforcer of the small town OMG to the biggest and baddest in the gang. It wasn't personal, it was strictly business and that's how it had to be. Plonczynski didn't write him a citation although he could have written several. Instead he chose to write several written warnings and gave the knife that was closer to a machete than a knife, back to the enforcer and allowed him to get back on the motorcycle and go along back to his life (Figure 13.1).

Figure 13.1 Renegade Outlaw Motorcycle Gang Member.

Years later, while conducting an investigation on social media, Plonczynski was able to find this individual again. He was still living in Florida, not too far from where all of the action was that one fateful night, but was now retired in good standing with the gang. He appeared to have a little bit of money and was living well with the woman who did tattoos for the gang. In pictures on social media he still had the gang's tattoos, which are indications that the subject is in good standing with the gang. Living as an enforcer nationally for any gang would mean that the person would have to travel a lot. They would have to be the biggest, they would have to be the baddest, and they would have to do everything they can to maintain that status in the gang. No one can live that lifestyle forever as there is always someone bigger and badder just around the corner.

Case Study #3

Sur 13 Home Invasion

During the early hours of September 5, 2006, members of Sur 13 had a gang meeting at a local leader's home. At this meeting numerous members were present. Among these members were Carlos and Hugo as well as female gang members such as Nora. While the members met to drink beer, and smoke cigarettes and marijuana, they discussed all of the problems that were currently taking place, such as a lack of guns and money. It was during this time that one of them decided that they had wanted to bring up a possible robbery for discussion. It's unknown exactly who initiated the conversation about the robbery, but it is well known who the members were that decided to take part in the home invasion robbery. After the gang decided on who was going to go and commit the crime, weapons were located and distributed to those that were going. Of the gang members that were going, their ages ranged between 14 and 17 years old. None of them had valid driver's licenses, but all were very well versed in driving. It was decided that Hugo, who had the most experience, would drive the gang members to the location, then circle in the area and wait to pick up. It was decided that Nora would be the distraction and the two other male gang members would aid her in robbing a trailer where numerous subjects were known to be living that allegedly were dealing in large levels of narcotics. At approximately 3:00 in the morning the gang members left the meeting area where they had spent much of their time that evening talking about how they were going to commit the crime, in addition to what they were going to look for and try to obtain. Hugo was able to borrow a vehicle, and along with the other gang members, was given a gun to carry in case there was a need to inflict violence or fear. Once the gang members had gone to the trailer park they exited the vehicle and Hugo promptly left the area. Nora and the other two male gang members put bandannas around their necks and covered themselves up as best they could with her clothing until the time was right and they would need to put them over their faces. The two male gang members quickly ran from the car to a location just outside of the doorway of the trailer, one having a shotgun, the other one having a handgun. Nora stood in front of the door waiting for the right time when she should knock on the door. Everything was set in place and ready to happen. One of the occupants of the trailer had gotten up and looked out the window and seen Nora. All of the occupants of the trailer were currently awake at this time. It was believed by law enforcement that there was actual narcotics in the trailer, however, in very small amounts, and not the amounts that the gang members themselves thought were present. The occupant of the trailer who observed Nora later told law enforcement that he had seen her and felt that she was out of place and that something was wrong. It was very soon after he had observed her outside of the window that Nora knocked on the door. The victim opened the door believing that she might be in need of something, even though he was well aware that she didn't belong in the trailer park, had not seen her before, and thought that something was wrong. As the door opened the two males who were positioned outside of the door quickly made entry with guns drawn and bandannas placed over their faces to conceal their identities. It was this point that Nora took her bandanna and placed it over her face as well, drew her gun, and charged in behind her fellow gang members. The three occupants of the trailer were ordered to the ground at gunpoint. All three gang members were shouting commands, some of them in confliction with what the other gang members were shouting. The one victim that had opened the door for Nora refused to get on the ground and instead elected to sit on the couch. He would later tell law enforcement it was like watching television. He couldn't believe it was real. Unknown to the gang members, there was a large black hole in this trailer where an AC unit would have a duct come into the trailer for cooling purposes. As the gang members made entry to the trailer, shouting and yelling, one would-be victim was able to escape through the hole and run towards a main road and the entrance to the trailer park. As he was able to make it to the entrance of the trailer park, it would just so happen that there was a zone unit patrolling the area for possible car burglaries. This deputy was quickly told that there was a robbery in progress at his friend's and law enforcement needed to hurry because they had guns. He pointed out the trailer to the deputy sheriff who then started to walk over to the trailer to see if there was any truth as to what he was being told. As it would happen the door was never closed behind Nora when she was the last one to come into the trailer. The door was found by the deputy to be slightly open by approximately two inches. As the deputy peered through the doorway, he observed the suspects and the robbery unfolding. He also observed one male with a shotgun pointed at the victims on the ground. The deputy then backed off seeking cover while calling in the armed home invasion to the dispatcher. As he backed off from the scene while the crime was taking place, at some point the suspects had to have realized he was there. They were told by one of the victims that they could flee out the back through the same hole that had just been used less than two minutes earlier for an escape. The suspects then fled out the hole. At some point, one of them contacted Hugo and explained that things had gone south very fast and that a pickup was needed at a predetermined location. Garments such as the blue bandannas and firearms were discarded along the way. Anything that would identify them to law enforcement as having been part of the crime was quickly discarded. One of the gang members lost a white Converse high top sneaker while he ran. One drawback for this would-be assailant was, as many gang members are known to do, they buy clothing which is too big. In this case the pants waistline was too big and he had no belt. He was therefore forced to at least use one hand to try and keep his pants up. At most they had gotten a couple dollars of cash, a pair of sunglasses, and some other frivolous items with little or no value. Law enforcement staged and then made entry to the trailer. As they did so the victims began opening the door, deputies were told that the suspects had fled through the hole on the other side of the trailer. Additional units were called to set up a perimeter and a description of all three suspects was quickly obtained and broadcast over the radio for responding units to watch for. Near the edge of the perimeter one of the deputies observed one of the Hispanic males jogging. As there were very few people out at this time in the morning and even fewer matching the description of the suspects, the 15-year-old gang member was taken down at gunpoint and arrested. He was placed in the back of the patrol car and brought back to the scene of the crime. Nearby a shotgun was located and seized as evidence. What was even more telling, was that this suspect only had one white high top Converse sneaker on. He had run out of the other one as he was escaping through the hole of the trailer. In all likelihood he never had his sneakers tied because that wouldn't be cool and as a result was forced to lose one sneaker and run with the other one still on his foot. When the deputy originally had seen him running, or jogging, the suspect let go of his pants in an attempt to swing his arms harder and faster to gain speed and distance between the deputy. As you can imagine, the result was that this suspect was forced to do what's called the Penguin, as his pants had dropped to his ankles limiting the distance between strides and making it easy for him to get captured. The other male and Nora were able to make it to Hugo, and were driven away from the crime scene in the same car that they had arrived in. Hugo immediately drove these would-be robbers to meet up with Carlos in a sort of debrief to explain what a taken place and what they were going to do now. When they met Carlos it was still early morning, however Carlos was still awake and most likely drunk and stoned. Carlos was a lieutenant at this time in the 17th St. clique of Sur 13. While he wasn't at the very top he was very well respected and extremely street-smart. Carlos took the guns that the gang members still had and as the following day was a school day, made sure that Hugo got them home so they could go to school. It was a sort of attempt to have an alibi in case law enforcement was able to get a confession from the one member that was arrested. Unknown to law enforcement at the time the one person that had just been arrested was also the weakest link. He had been in the gang for the shortest amount of time, knew the other members less, and had had no previous encounters with law enforcement. As many in law enforcement will tell you, that's the exact type of gang member that you want to have an interview with. Hard-core gang members that have been in the system countless times often don't talk. These gang members are some of the more blood boiling people in our society to deal with. As law enforcement will talk to them they'll either say nothing, lie, or just plain insult you. This wasn't the case here though. This gang member was driven back to the scene of the crime and positively identified by at least two of the victims of the robbery. As an arrest was made the Gang Units for Manatee County and for Bradenton Police Department were never notified that night and it wasn't until the following morning as a matter of fact that the Manatee County Sheriff's Office Gang Unit was notified. The crime scene unit was requested and latent fingerprint examinations were later requested for all of the fingerprints that were pulled at the scene of the crime. In the corresponding report deputies made sure to note that the size of the Converse sneaker that was located in the trailer was the size and color of the Converse sneaker that was still on the suspect. Deputy Plonczynski researched the past criminal history for the arrested juvenile. As the suspect was so young, there was nothing to find. He first made contact with the juvenile's mother and spoke to her at length over the phone. She was a good, hard-working woman, and a single parent that was trying to control her children. There had been no male role model in the house and in between working full time and trying to keep a stable home, she was doing everything that she could. This is often seen in the gang world, and is a common theme. A broken home, with little or no parental oversight, and lots of spare time on a juvenile's hand. After speaking to the mother at length, Detective Plonczynski was able to get her to agree to allow him to speak to her son. Detective Plonczynski then went to the juvenile detention center and post-Miranda spoke to the offender. Plonczynski didn't try to intimidate him, he didn't come down as the tough cop, or appear threatening in any way. Instead he played just the opposite and tried to explain to the boy that this is what happens when you join a criminal street gang. The other gang members were not going to be helping him, they were not going to be supportive in any way, and they were not going to be there for him now. Instead he was there in the juvenile detention center for minimum of 21 days in secure detention on his own. Plonczynski also told him, that since he had been identified by two of the victims, in addition to having a sneaker that matched another sneaker at the scene of the crime, that this was an open and shut case essentially. Plonczynski also informed this not so tough gang member that because of the violence and the guns that were used, that this juvenile may be tried as an adult. That being the case, this 15-year-old may be looking at going to adult prison. It wasn't right that he take the rap for the others involved. Plonczynski didn't make any promises, but he did say that if the juvenile was willing to work with him, that he would be willing to go in front of the judge and explain that the juvenile had tried to do right in the end. Very often in court, judges and prosecutors look for people who have been found guilty to have some sort of remorse, in this case helping law enforcement track down the other gang members who were involved in the crime would help to show that he had known that he had made a mistake and was trying to do right by it. What Plonczynski really knew, was that if this gang member did snitched on the others he most likely wouldn't be in the gang very long. Plonczynski conducted a photo pack line up of several other individuals he believed may have been involved in this crime. The gang member quickly confessed to the crime and implicated Hugo as the driver and positively identified the other male gang member who committed the crime with them. Plonczynski was shocked to find out that Nora was the female involved as he had known Nora from past experiences but did not believe that she had risen to this level of violence or criminal activity. After leaving the juvenile detention center and having obtained the confession, Plonczynski started to return to the Sheriff's Office. While en route, he received a phone call from a school principal. The school principal had said that one of her students had come to see her earlier that morning. It was during that time that he confessed to her that he had been a part of this crime. Plonczynski turned the car around and quickly headed to the school. Once there he got the parents information and contacted the student's mother. He explained in fine detail what had occurred and asked permission to interview her son post-Miranda. After obtaining permission, he spoke to the juvenile. This gang member had been in the gang for a bit longer but still was extremely new the criminal justice system. Morally he knew the difference between right and wrong. But as is often the case when drugs and alcohol are present, people often do things that they normally wouldn't. When it comes to gang member's, drugs and alcohol are almost always present and therefore rationality is usually thrown by the wayside. Plonczynski was able to obtain a full confession at the school and arrested this gang member. After dropping them off at the juvenile detention center he then went to the juvenile's home and asked permission to go into the child's bedroom. Once inside the bedroom he located and seized numerous gang-related items, which, under Florida law, may be seized even if they don't pertain to the crime itself. Unfortunately, no guns were located or other evidence that supported that this juvenile was part of the crime.

Plonczynski made contact with Dutch. He explained to Dutch what was going on, the facts of the case, and asked for help as this case seemed to be getting larger and larger by the moment. Dutch was a seasoned veteran on the force as a detective, and well-versed in the gang world. Dutch then went to the juvenile detention center and after once again speaking to the juvenile's mother, spoke to the gang member that was originally arrested not far from the crime scene. It was during this interview that he was able to obtain information from the juvenile on what happened to the guns. Dutch learned that after Hugo had picked up the other gang members he had driven them to see Carlos and Carlos had taken the guns to another gang member's house. It was the same gang member's house where these gang members had been partying just prior to committing the crime. However, due to the fact that this information was relatively hearsay, it would be impossible to obtain a search warrant for the home in order to search for these guns. It was approximately two days after this that Nora, Hugo and Carlos were all arrested on warrants that had been obtained in reference to violations of probation. Many of the members of this clique of Sur 13 were on juvenile probation. To violate the probation was relatively easy. Not going to school, not attending class, and other such things like being away from the home without a parent or guardian were all violations of probation. It often only took obtaining the juvenile's class history to see that after several days of being on probation, many of these gang members were in violation because they simply didn't want to go to school or go to class. Once Carlos was arrest, he was brought to the Bradenton Police Department. Once there his mother refused to allow law enforcement to speak to him. Pieper and Plonczynski met with Hugo's mother and spoke to her about her son's involvement, or at least the part that they were aware of. As was always the case with Hugo's mother she was a good parent and a good member of the community. She was always the parent that gave permission for law enforcement to speak to her son. When Pieper and Plonczynski would go to her door, the first thing out of their mouths would always be to ask, how she was feeling and how she was doing health wise. She never once gave them any reason to think that she was anything other than an outstanding person overall. Once again, this was a broken home with several children in the household ranging from toddler to late teenager. The toddlers were her grandchildren. Pieper and Plonczynski interviewed Hugo about Nora and the other gang members who were believed to be involved. They also had recently learned that the first gang member who was arrested on the perimeter went by the street name "Payaso." Hugo was true to form this day like he had been every other time that Plonczynski and Pieper had ran into him and as he always would be in the future, and he didn't say anything that would help investigators learn further information or other details pertaining to this crime. After saying that he didn't know who Nora was, that he didn't know who Payaso was, or any other gang members whose names were brought up during the interview, he quickly invoked his right to remain silent and requested an attorney. That being the case there was no further interview after the juveniles were transported to the juvenile detention facility. Plonczynski and Pieper contacted Hugo's mother and asked her if it would be okay if they went to her house and searched his room. She agreed to allow the search. Hugo didn't have much. There was a mattress on the floor with a sheet and a pillow, clothing that had been neatly folded in a corner by his mother and left there, or thrown around the room after it had been used by Hugo. There was no dresser but there were items in the closet. A search of the bedroom was conducted while Hugo's mother stood present inside of the room. It was during this time that Plonczynski located a cell phone. Plonczynski asked Hugo's mother who this phone belonged to. She had stated that it was her phone, however Hugo was the only one that used it. Plonczynski stated that since it was her phone, would she mind if he looked through it for recently called phone numbers or text messages. Hugo's mother always true to form quickly gave permission without hesitation. Plonczynski started looking through the phone and upon opening the flip phone, observed the word "Sur 13." Plonczynski knew that he was on the right track. Under the gang name on the screen of the phone was also Hugo's gang name, which was "Gloom." Anyone who had been investigating gangs for any length of time knew that Hugo's street name was Gloom. Outside of Hugo's residence, one could find the name tagged on almost every building, staircase, and dumpster in the apartment complex. Inside of the recent calls folder was a who's who of gang members and their phone numbers. Plonczynski quickly wrote down who the gang members were, their phone numbers, and the times they were called on the days before and after the home invasion. Plonczynski was able to locate the 17th St. gang leader's home phone number and called it. He wasn't able to speak to the gang leader himself, however he was greeted by a rap song where the gang leader was wrapping about committing violent crimes, such as murder. Plonczynski was asked after several long minutes of this horrible music to leave a message. It was at that time that he told the gang leader who he was, why he was calling and told him to have a nice day. Further investigation of the phone showed Hugo to be a liar. He told investigators that he didn't know anyone with the name Nora, or Payaso, or any of the other gang members that were known to be in his clique. Instead, many of the gang members that had been mentioned to Hugo had both their names and phone numbers in this phone. Since Hugos mother did not use the phone, she was more then happy to give it to investigators. She was a good mother who rewarded her children whenever she could, however Hugo was the one child that she was never able to get turned in the right direction. Years later, she would move Hugo out to Oklahoma in hopes of removing him from the gang lifestyle that he had grown up in. However, by that time it was already too late. Maybe if she had moved him out there sooner or Hugo had been born a decade or two earlier things would've worked out by going to Oklahoma. However due to social media, Hugo was able to maintain his connection to the gang even over vast distances and would later return to Bradenton and further his criminal lifestyle.

As the days and weeks followed, the state attorney's office quickly made contact with all of the investigators involved. The case, for all its strengths, had numerous weaknesses. With the exception of the original arrest made, the remaining arrests were all based in probable cause through co-conspirator statements. The state attorney was extremely uneasy about putting gang members on the witness stand and having them testify about other gang member's involvement. This is a common theme in any gang investigation whereby a prosecutor will do many things if not anything to avoid putting a gang member on the stand. This is not to say that this is a bad way of doing business, and many in law enforcement totally understand. You see gang members, when they get on the stand, are no different than when they're out in the streets. Often lies are the reality, and on the streets these lies really don't amount to much except big talk. However, on the stand in a court-room, in front of a jury with opposing counsel able to question your witness, it's a whole different world. These lies quickly get unraveled by an opposing attorney and gang members often look like fools in front of a jury. Plonczyn-ski requested to contact the victims and get phone numbers so that sub-poenas could be issued immediately. The state attorney had agreed to press charges in the case originally against all the juveniles. Anyone familiar with the criminal justice system knows that juvenile court and adult court are very different in several ways. In Florida, juvenile court consists of a judge who also acts as the jury. Looking back and doing a Monday morning quar-terback review of the case in its entirety, Plonczynski believed that he made a mistake in pushing to have the juveniles tried as adults. It would've been easier to obtain convictions in juvenile court, even if the sentences might not have been as severe. After consulting with Dutch and Pieper, Carlos was charged as an accessory after the fact for having taken the firearms from the gang members just after the botched crime occurred. Plonczynski and his partner at the time worked nonstop at trying to locate the victims that iden-tified the gang member, who had been arrested on the perimeter. This was the gang member who investigators later learned to be Payaso. Plonczynski later found the victims and was able to have them served subpoenas in order for depositions to occur. Moreover, he was able to do photo pack line ups with the victims, whereby one victim was able to identify Nora, however the other victim was unable to do so. Coupled with the fact that these victims were also drug users and lived the drug-user lifestyle, didn't make it any easier for the state attorney to work the case and obtain justice. In the end, only the two boys who had given full confessions received any sentences. Nora, Hugo, and Carlos were all arrested and charged as adults with corresponding crimes to their actions for that night. All were taken to the Manatee County jail and housed as adults. However, none of the three were ever found guilty. In the criminal histories of these three, were numerous other crimes. As a juvenile alone, Carlos was charged 23 times. Carrying a concealed firearm, aggravated assault with a deadly weapon, use of a firearm within 1000 feet of a roadway, battery on a school board employee, several burglaries, in addition to numerous other crimes. This was just a hint of what was yet to come with Carlos and Hugo. These crimes would later become the predicate acts for which they would be charged in one of Plonczynski's two largest cases of his career. The first case was titled Operation: Tidal Wave. The second case was subsequently titled Operation: Receding Water. Both of these cases were charges filed by the Office of the Statewide Prosecutor in Tampa, Florida as racketeering cases.

Case Study #4

Sur 13 R.I.C.O. Operation: Tidal Wave

On January 24, 2007, Detective Plonczynski along with numerous other deputy sheriffs from the Manatee County Sheriff's Office (MSO) and outside help from various other agencies to include Pieper and the Bradenton Police Department, sought out to use a law created back in 1974, against local area gangs that would later become a sledge hammer in the prosecution of gangs and gang members in Manatee County nationwide. The Florida Department of Law Enforcement (FDLE) had come to the Manatee County Sheriff's Office originally with the idea of doing this type of investigation. Operation: Tidal Wave would mark the second time that MSO, BPD, and FDLE had come together to conduct such an investigation. Prior to this date, the Manatee County Sheriff's Office in conjunction with the Florida Department of Law Enforcement had already done a Racketeer Influenced and Corrupt Organization (R.I.C.O.) case against the criminal street gang Brown Pride Loco's (BPL). This investigation would be into the criminal street gang Sur 13.

Originally, when conceived, there were numerous gang members from three different gangs involved as suspects. During this time in Manatee County, three gangs were at war with the Brown Pride Locos. These three gangs were forming an alliance with each other called Trece Unidos (three united): Sur 13, Mara Salvatrucha 13 and the West Side Locos (Figure 13.2).

During this time, drive-by shootings and the firebombing of vehicles within Bradenton's jurisdiction sky rocketed. These crimes were done as gang initiations as membership in gangs rose. It was around this time that the Internet was in its infancy for the most part. MySpace.com was the main location where people went to connect online. Facebook was hardly known and was not even a social network that had been checked for any footprints online of these gang members.

Figure 13.2 Sur 13, West Side Locos, and MS-13 Graffiti.

For a case of this magnitude, local law enforcers, have to find someone who is going to prosecute what would turn out to be a monster of a case. For cases of this nature the local state attorney's office explained that they did not have the manpower to be able to throw at this case, as the current caseload at that time for all assistant state attorney's was massive. Nothing has changed to this day in that regard. As a result, the Office of the Statewide Prosecutor was sought out to help both the Florida Department of Law enforcement and the Manatee County Sheriff's Office to bring this case to a court. Due to the fact that there were very few predicated crimes outside of the jurisdiction of the 12th judicial circuit in which Manatee County lay, the statewide prosecutor went to the State Attorney's Office and respectfully requested to be sworn in as prosecutors under the local state attorney for jurisdiction. This type of action was a no-brainer and a win-win for everybody.

The first question became who is going to be arrested? This is not a question to be quickly thought out and would take months to answer. Criminal histories would have to be ran and reports would have to be pulled. Originally, Plonczynski had wanted approximately 15–20 people to be suspects in this investigation, with the knowledge that this investigation encompassed approximately 150–200 people who are associated with the most hard-core of gang members in the county at that time. In the end, the number 14 was determined to be the final number for arrest warrants. It was picked for several reasons, the first being a slap in the face to any gang that use

Strike force swoops in on SUR-13

Figure 13.3 Operation: Tidal Wave Hits the Paper.

the number 13, as 14 is often seen as a rival. Moreover, any more than 14 subjects arrested would create a mountain of additional work that would need to be done. The strain of arresting, investigating, and convicting 14 gang members is no small task. Ask any investigator who has conducted a racketeering case and they will tell you that the more gang members you have, the more difficult and harder a prosecution will become. Just looking forward to any racketeering case and outlying some of the initial problems can be tumultuous. Just the thought of being in deposition with 14 defense attorneys alone for eight hours at a time, can even make the most hardened and well-seasoned detective cringe and walk right out the door and never look back (Figure 13.3).

During this targeting process, Pieper was asked to assist in their arrest selections. Target selection in a case such as as this, can be exciting as well as frustrating. Just as everyone from the prosecutor on down had begun to settle on the targets, Pieper would come in almost daily, with his two cents on more gang members to look at and go after. It was maddening at times. With every new target that Pieper threw at the other investigators involved in the case, he was shot down for one reason or another. "He's too young," or "He doesn't have the predicate acts," they would tell him. Now mind you, there were already great targets that did make the final list that were later arrested, that were in the city of Bradenton's jurisdiction, but Pieper always had to get one more in and was never satisfied. He was dedicated to a fault at trying to target more of Bradenton P.D.'s problem children rather than leaving the target list alone.

In Manatee County, a gang leader had recently passed away. He was well known and respected on the streets as well as feared. His brother had recently been a suspect in an aggravated battery-attempted murder in Sarasota County, and as such was quickly added to the list of suspects to be arrested on these charges. Another person who made the list, was "Speedy." While this individual had never really plagued the counties gang task force, he had been a big-time player behind the scenes, in a lot of what was occurring in the county and was a very big player in the city of Bradenton's jurisdiction. It was requested from Pieper that he be placed on the list and after some discussion, Speedy was added to the list. Carlos was also placed on this list. Moreover, during the investigation, Plonczynski had gone to a local convention center for a gun show. In the south, just like everywhere else in the nation, gun shows are pretty prevalent. In this case, there were gang members out in the parking lot. Plonczynski had gone to the gun show unarmed due to the fact that you're not allowed to enter the gun show with a firearm if you are not on duty as law enforcement. Knowing that he would just have to give over his gun or have the ammunition taken away from him and have the firearm zip tied, he chose not to bring a firearm. As luck would have it, this was a mistake that day. As he entered the convention parking area and walked away from his car, he observed a group of approximately six 13 gang members. These gang members were standing in a group smoking cigarettes and talking to one another at the bumper area of one of their cars. As Plonczynski walked by unafraid, he said hello in a general kind of way to all of them. He had known all of them by face and by name having dealt with all of them numerous times in the past. As Plonczynski would learn, this was one of many mistakes in dealing with gang members. After he had said hello, he was told by these gang members to keep walking as they were going to kick his ass once he got inside of the gun show. Plonczynski continued to walk towards the front doors without saying another word. The gang members however continued to laugh and mock him as he walked away. The distance from the car where the incident took place to the front door was approximately 50 yards. Every 5–10 yards Plonczynski would look over his shoulder to see if they were running up on him or not. He made it to the front door and inside the gun show. Once inside and seeing a Palmetto Police Officer, he quickly explained what had just transpired. He then made his way to a gun dealer and purchased both a new gun and ammunition. He waited some time to see if the gang members came in after him. They did attempt to do so, however they were stopped at the door by the Palmetto Police Department and told that they were not going to be allowed to come in. This action actually might've saved his life. If it wasn't for the quick actions of the Palmetto Police Department, and officer Chad Oyler, the day could have ended far worse for Plonczynski. After some time in the gun show Plonczynski walked out the front doors to his car with Chad Oyler in tow. As such Plonczynski later went back and wrote a report in reference to assault on a law enforcement officer which would later become a predicate offense for this racketeering case. This incident is just one small sample of the dangers that are hidden out there. As such it fits well that some of the gang members involved in this incident were arrested for racketeering. It was meant to send a message, a message that probably fell on deaf ears (Figure 13.4).

Throughout this investigation there were several crimes and incidents that occurred that grabbed investigators ears. One event occurred that Pieper would not let pass them by. Pieper had developed an informant that was able to provide information on many of the gang initiation jump-ins, several fire bombings, and other crimes that Tres Unitos were conducting. Pieper was able to get a search warrant for the "Dough Boy's" house. The "Dough Boy" was the leader of the local MS-13 set and was on orders from his family members in Los Angeles to start up the gang in Bradenton.

Figure 13.4 Gang Warning about What Happens to Law Enforcement Here.

Pieper's informant stated that the Dough Boy had obtained a gun to protect himself to protect himself from rival gang members. Dough Boy was Latino but lived in a predominately black neighborhood and racial tensions were building because the community knew that it was his gang that had recently killed a innocent nine-year-old child. According to Pieper's informant, Dough Boy had a gun in his bed room. Now the Dough Boy was still a juvenile. He had previously attacked Pieper on school grounds and his propensity for violence was well documented. Law enforcement was able to learn that Dough Boy wanted to shoot Pieper's informant in the leg, allegedly to see if the gun actually worked. Shooting the gun into the air, ground or even an abandoned house wasn't good enough for the Dough Boy, it had to be in the leg of Pieper's informant.

Based on this information Pieper was able to obtain a search warrant for the Dough Boy's residence. Before hitting the residence, Pieper met with Ski and they had a meeting. Pieper stressed the importance of this situation to Ski and added that because of the potential for further violence even after a possible arrest and conviction, this gang member would only become worse. As a result, lots of overtime came in to play and a full work-up and historical investigation was done on Dough Boy to see if he could be added to the R.I.C.O. By adding him, another gang member would have to be removed. However, due to the circumstances that existed, everyone understood. Pieper and the BPD SWAT team hit the Dough Boy's residence with Ski in tow. Just as planned there were several Sur 13 and MS-13 gang members present when they hit the house.

During a search of the residence Pieper and Ski located the firearm exactly where Pieper's informant had stated it would be. Amongst some of the other items that were located was an MS-13 "bible" which explained the rules and traditions of the gang (a very damning piece of evidence proving gang involvement). They also discovered an entire dresser that contained rival Norte 14 clothes that Dough Boy would wear when out "running missions." This was unreal and never in the history of gang investigations had this been heard of. This group would intentionally wear rival gang colors when out committing crimes. When witnesses gave statements, law enforcement would automatically be thrown off the trail due to the colors being worn. It really was one hell of a smart "red herring." In this case, the situation could not have worked out better. Now for the tricky part, get the R.I.C.O. warrant for the Dough Boy completed before he could bond out of jail.

As time was approaching the round up date, pressure and excitement was mounting. The troops were excited to kick this party off. It had been some time since investigators had been able to go after this many high level threats to the community.

After everything had been put together and the warrants for the arrest of the suspects had been made, it was sit and wait time. The Sheriff wanted to do a press conference on the day of the warrants sweep and man power needed to be put in place as well as all the logistics of interrogations post arrest and so on. It was the night before the round up and Pieper had to work until midnight. They were meeting at Manatee County Sheriff's Office at 5:00 am. Plonczynski was "holding" on to all of the arrest warrants, so that if the targets got stopped the night before, they would not get arrested and then start a chain of phone calls and alert the other gang members. At about 22:30 hours, Plonczynski got a call from Pieper saying that he was out with Speedy and Speedy had just invited him to his wedding, that was scheduled to be held in two weeks. Pieper was having a hard time containing himself. Pieper had known of the wedding for quite some time and had planned on being there, or near there, in an undercover capacity videotaping it for documentation purposes. It was insanity to think he was actually invited. It would be a wedding day Pieper would never see. Pieper call Plonczynski and begged to take Speedy into custody. He knew however, without permission if word leaked about the warrants sweep, in the morning things could get ugly. Plonczynski wasn't hot on the idea. It wasn't like Speedy wasn't going to be in his bed the next morning or anything. Plonczynski made a call to the prosecutor in the case to get a second opinion. Both agreed, 0500 hours was close but not that close, they agreed to tell Pieper to take a deep breath and keep cool. Speedy was one of the many caught July 7th 2007. Pieper had been asked to remain at the command post. After Speedys arrest, Pieper went and met him to personally conduct the interview. Speedy knew the jig was up and gave the only confession that day. He would later go on to be the state's key witness. As such, Speedy was able to get one of the best deals when it came to sentencing. Several years later, after his release from prison, both Pieper and Plonczynski would routinely check in on him. For a while, it may have been this constant checking in with law enforcement that kept him on the side of righteousness. However just as a zebra cannot change its stripes, Speedy later reverted back to the lifestyle he had known and grown up in. He would be stopped at a traffic stop, where he was the driver. In the car were other suspected gang members, along with a shotgun and various ammunition. It appeared to investigators that this crew was going out to conduct a drive-by shooting that evening, although it was never confirmed. Speedy would later go back for a violation of probation to prison. Where he remains at the time of this writing.

This investigation was comprised of numerous different cliques inside of Sur 13. The arrests included one female among the 14 and two juveniles (Figure 13.5).

Figure 13.5 Pure Sureno.

In the original 14 arrests, one of the Sur 13 members who pled guilty to racketeering and conspiracy to commit racketeering was Samuel Campos Conde. Conde was the first to plead guilty to the charges of this investigation, and as such had one of the lighter sentences. Since his original arrest and sentencing, Conde was released from the Florida State prison. After which Conde did return to his association with other criminal street gang members. On the night of his murder, he was with another documented criminal street gang member just prior to being shot and killed in a shootout. It is rumored that he was killed by a rival gang member, however that murder investigation is currently still unsolved. Several of the gang members have since been released from the Department of Corrections for their sentences and were put on probation. These gang members have violated numerous times and yet still remain on probation. One gang member, who was arrested under the original racketeering investigation, in the Island Bound Surenos clique of Sur 13, was arrested several times for a violation of probations. The judge however just kept giving him more and more probation. It was disgraceful how the courts would just let him back out over and over again. For example, several times he was drug tested and came back "hot" for cocaine or marijuana. Other times this gang member would take off his ankle GPS bracelet and go who knows where. The judge was always the same judge and very liberal. However, this gang member committed a new law violation of rape and subsequently violation of probation. He was convicted of this violation of probation and sentenced to over 25 years in the Florida Department of Corrections. The same gang member had admitted during his proffer after being arrested for racketeering, to the murder of Travis Pompei. He went to trial for the murder charge originally, but was found not guilty by a jury. It was often the subject of conjecture between Pieper and Plonczynski that a member of the jury had been a friend of the defendant and thusly no conviction was ever made. Either way it was a fitting end to how this gang member will live out the remainder of his life. However, it was also a painful lesson that shows that even if you do have subjects arrested for 1st degree felonies such as racketeering, that without a judge that understands what a threat these people are at sentencing both for the original charge and subsequent violations of probations after they are released from the Department of Corrections, that anything can still happen once they are released back in to society. Liberal courts and liberal judges are too often the problem in cases such as this one.

Javier was also one of the original members arrested for violation of the R.I.C.O. act. Javier had just committed murder in a shootout with rival gang members for which he had already been arrested. In this case, the state offered him 10 years plus probation if he pled guilty early and upfront. Knowing that the murder was a slam-dunk, there was really no bang for the buck to try and prosecute him further for the homicide. As a result, he pled guilty to racketeering after having just been found guilty for murder. In the murder trial, he was given life without the possibility of parole, and therefore no sentence for racketeering or conspiracy to commit racketeering would have trumped the murder sentence.

Once all of the arrests and sentencing for this investigation were completed, both Pieper and Plonczynski sat back down and started again. The original investigation had been titled Operation: Tidal Wave. In this case, they decided to call the subsequent investigation Operation: Receding Waters. While the second racketeering case was just as much a success as the first, it goes on to this day, as two of the subjects are still fugitives from justice and have not been caught (Figure 13.6).

Figure 13.6 Hugo Post R.I.C.O. Arrest.

Case Study #5

Nino: The Final Chapter

As things— were happening in Manatee County, things were happening elsewhere as well. As it would turn out one night both Pelone and Gordo were in Tampa with another gang member. All three were documented gang members and out looking for trouble later that night. As they drove in a remote part of town, they found several individuals on the side of the road, attempting to fix their car. Never wanting to miss an opportunity, gang members will strike at anything when money is involved and these gang members decided that they were going to in fact commit a robbery. They were armed and pulled over pretending to want to help. As they approached, they spoke to the victims and explained that they wanted to help. As they got close however to the individuals, a gun was pulled and things quickly changed. As luck would have it there wasn't much to take. The gang members took whatever they could and fled the scene. The victims however called law enforcement who actually were pretty close and able to locate the getaway car relatively quickly. A felony takedown was conducted by the Hillsboro County Sheriff's Office, at which point Lucky fled from the traffic stop. Deputies gave chase and ended up having to fight and taze him prior to being handcuffed and detained. Moreover, when arrested he still had a gun in his possession. A show up was conducted with the victims who positively identified these individuals as having been the suspects who had committed the robbery. Plonczynski and Pieper both learned about the incident and were ecstatic. This is a major crime that these two well-known Manatee County gang members had committed in another jurisdiction where the victims were unaware of these gang ties and most likely would not be deterred or scared off from testifying. The state attorney's office in Hillsboro decided to direct file at the last second on Gordo and Pelone (who were juveniles), however the paperwork was late in getting to the detention center. After 21 days the juveniles were released prior to them being taken to the adult jail. Manatee County Sheriff's Office and Bradenton Police Department were both put on notice and requested by the Hillsboro County state attorney's office to locate these individuals. Warrants were immediately placed into the system for their arrest. Neither Plonczynski nor Pieper believed however that they would be able to find the individuals as both had strong ties outside of the county and most likely new that if caught or captured that they would be facing a lengthy sentence. As it turned out, this act in conjunction with their priors gave Plonczynski enough incentive to move forward and request that the statewide prosecutor charge these individuals with violations of the racketeering statute. Now that these gang members have been charged as adults for this case it would be easy to charge them in a racketeering case as adults as well. The only problem was that both were now on the run. It was approximately three months later when Plonczynski was in his unmarked car driving home. It'd been a long day but he was in full uniform, tired and hungry. He was on University Parkway about to turn into a strip mall with numerous other vehicles one evening. The lane directly to his left was also a turn lane to go into the strip mall, and the beat-up SUV next to him that was only slightly forward of where he was stopped, had music blaring from it. Annoyed, it got Plonczynski's attention even if he couldn't do anything about it at the time. As he looked at the vehicle, the back seat passenger rolled the window down and spit directly onto Plonczynski's unmarked police vehicle. The subject who had done it laughed, turned around and looked at Plonczynski. Deer in the headlights is an understatement for how wide Nino's eyes became. He went from laughing to sheer horror upon seeing who was driving the car that he had just spit on. Plonczynski's heart immediately started to race, and he got on the radio to the dispatcher stating that he needed radio silence except for him. He added that he had an armed robbery suspect directly in front of him and needed immediate backup to his location. The light turned green where the two vehicles had been stopped and the window quickly went up where Nino had been sitting. Plonczynski knew immediately that this was going to be a foot chase and he was weighted down very heavily by all of the equipment. To anyone who's never ran with a gun, extra magazines, handcuffs, OC spray, a flashlight, and a radio in addition to full body armor and in boots, let me just say that the bad guy has a distinct advantage in any foot chase. Plonczynski knew that there had to be other subjects in the car as well. One of them may have been another individual with a warrant and Plonczynski believed that the two were going to be gang members. This put him at a distinct disadvantage. But taking the chance was part of the job and something that any law enforcement officer would have done. The location of the traffic stop was on the Manatee County, Sarasota County line. Thusly backup typically isn't as close as it would have been, had the stop been done in a different working patrol zone. As the cars move forward Plonczynski activated his lights and siren and thought about literally hitting the car and pushing it off the roadway if it didn't stop. This is not what is typically known as a safe maneuver. What Plonczynski was thinking here was literally taking his car side-by-side and just pushing it off the road. It would've been a very dangerous maneuver and potentially Plonczynski may have gotten time off if things had gone wrong. As luck would have it however, the car actually stopped immediately after making a left-hand turn into the strip mall. Plonczynski parked his car at the back passenger quarter panel, blocking traffic in one lane with his vehicle and immediately jumped out of his car. Sirens could be heard way off in the distance, however Plonczynski at least knew that they were coming. Plonczynski then ran to the door where he knew Nino had been sitting. He then nearly ripped the door off the hinges when he opened it, extremely hyped up with adrenaline. The car was a piece of junk. As he opened the door he could see the passenger in the front seat turning around to look and see what was going on. The driver had also turned around to see why the door was opening. Straight ahead of Plonczynski in the back seat, was Pelone. Pelone was doing everything he could to open his door and escape. He must've tried to open the door by using the handle five or six times in quick repetition while Plonczynski was opening the door and surveying what was going on. Not waiting for Nino or anyone else to pull a gun or weapon, Plonczynski lunged inside of the vehicle and grabbed him by the foot. He then dragged him across the back seat of the car and threw him to the ground. He quickly picked him up and handcuffed him before Nino even knew what had occurred. Plonczynski then pushed Nino against the back of the SUV with his left hand holding him in place and with his right hand he had drawn his trusty Sig Sauer P220 handgun and pointed it directly at the occupants of the vehicle. He told them not to move and to stay where they were. In the meantime dispatch of been trying to reach Plonczynski over the radio to find out what his status was and get updates. The last time they had heard anything he only said that he was stopping a vehicle with an armed robbery suspect and gave a broad location of where he might be. Luckily enough there were lights and siren on his unmarked vehicle and both of them were still going off, which in this part of town was extremely distinctive. Backup quickly arrived, including a major in Plonczynski's agency, who came racing to Plonczynski's aid. Other deputies soon arrived and took custody of Nino. Plonczynski interviewed the remaining individuals in the car who, surprisingly enough, were not gang members. They were the coworkers of the local restaurant where Nino had been working. He had told everybody there that he was 21 and had been working for well over a month at this location, never having even filled out an application. He'd told the manager he was going to give them the information for the application, and never had. After hours he would drink at the bar because the people there believed he was over 21. In truth Nino didn't look a day over 12. Plonczynski allowed the coworkers to leave after a lengthy discussion of what had occurred. Plonczynski quickly learned that these gentlemen hadn't known Nino that long and were only giving him a ride as he had no car to get to work. So after Plonczynski learned this, he quickly did a follow-up investigation at the large chain restaurant and put them on notice of the illegalities of allowing a person such as Nino to work there, much less the danger they allowed by having such a person working for them without doing any kind of proper background check or proper paperwork. It was an amazing catch. Nino was booked into the Manatee County Sheriff's Office jail and that evening Plonczynski made contact with the Hillsboro County state attorney's office to notify them that the warrant had been served and the circumstances surrounding the arrest. Post arrest Plonczynski spoke to Nino. Nino blamed Plonczynski for everything that it happened in his life, not taking any responsibility for any of the problems that happened to him over the course of the last several years. Miraculously enough, this one law enforcement officer was the reason for all of Nino's problems. Nino told Plonczynski that his mother had fled the country after violating her probation and not wanting to go to prison. She was now somewhere in Mexico and only spoke to Nino once a month. She refused to come back to the United States knowing that she very well could face prison time and then deportation. Plonczynski thought it was funny that one law enforcement officer could be blamed for everything wrong in one person's life, but here was Nino saying just that. Later, after Nino had been transferred to Hillsboro and the robbery case went to trial. Plonczynski had been subpoenaed to testify at sentencing after Nino had been found guilty of the robbery. Plonczynski testified that Nino had been a documented gang member and discussed all of the different encounters he had with Nino and one of his co-conspirators in the robbery. Nino decided to have other gang members speak on his behalf at sentencing. In the end, justice prevailed here and Nino was sentenced to 25 years in the Florida Department of Corrections. After which, Immigration and Customs Enforcement then put a detainer on him for deportation after he had served his time. It was a fitting end to someone who had caused so many issues as part of the gang, in a community ravaged by gangs. What was interesting here however was that Lucky, didn't get the same punishment as Nino. For some reason, the judge took mercy on Lucky, and only sentenced him to 10 years. As Lucky was a natural born citizen in the United States, he didn't face the potential for deportation. As a result of this crime, Plonczynski was able to use it as a predicate act under R.I.C.O. and also charged Lucky with the racketeering statute. Lucky had been given 10 years DOC by the judge. In the end, Lucky pled guilty to racketeering. As such he worked out a plea agreement with the state and was sentenced to 15 years in the Department of Corrections. Considering that he was most likely the mastermind of the robbery, and a bigger threat to the community than Nino, it doesn't seem fitting that he got the lesser sentence, but thats the world we live in.

14 Strain to the Criminal Justice System

The US Department of Justice has released a report that states the growth of criminal gangs is increasing in all socio-economic areas of the country. According to The National Youth Gang Survey Office of Juvenile Justice and Delinquency Prevention (OJJDP) there were an estimated 28,100 gangs and 731,000 gang members throughout 3,500 jurisdictions nationwide. The prevalence rate of gang activity increased to 34.5% from 32.4%. Larger cities and suburban counties accounted for more than 96% of all gang homicides (Figure 14.1).

Robert Brzenchek interviewed Dale Yeager on the gang issue and the strain to the Criminal Justice System. Dale is a federally trained Forensic Profiler with the firm SERAPH of which Brzenchek sits on the board. Yeager stated, "Gangs need

Figure 14.1 House with Graffiti.

to be viewed differently by everyone. Gangs are not structured in the same way as they were 10 or even 15 years ago. Traditional gangs are still prominent, but they are now being teamed with international drug cartels, terrorist groups and even political groups domestically." We, meaning the law enforcement and intelligence communities, need to redefine gangs as domestic terrorist organizations because of these developments. "Now we have political/social justice groups who are deploying or tacitly encouraging violence against political structures and corporate structures in an attempt to bring about violent change. Traditional street gangs have been a part of this from their involvement in protests against white supremacy groups to the Black Lives Matter movement of today. The police intelligence departments must expand their fact gathering to understand these developments. I have taught in my federal classes that this violence by Leftist groups would increase and it has. Law enforcement agencies must use a different approach in gang interdiction; they must have a Task Force with state and Federal partners. The entire paradigm to fight gangs must be flipped on its head." "In law enforcement—Criminal Justice worlds we cannot worry about fallout or criticism from these groups. When public safety is involved we must be dispassionate and objective and provide the information that protects society from violence."

15 The Way Forward

As a doctoral researcher, Brzenchek researches real-world solutions to an age-old problem; gangs. He posits that the role of leaders in criminal justice reform cannot be over emphasized; it can impact the organizational structure and influence change. When criminal justice leaders are aware of their roles and what is expected of them, they are able to make better choices (Schechter, 2012). According to Gadeken (2012), leaders should focus on building leadership capacity and offering support for new and struggling staff to help them to achieve their maximum potential. In building leadership, team leaders will help to increase the skills as leaders (Loertscher, 2008b). It is crucial for leaders to use their expertise and experience to build and boost programs such as PGPs (Loertscher, 2005). In doing this it is important to provide adequate professional assistance through regular staff development sessions, including external workshops or bringing in resource persons. According to DuFour (2018) these efforts will ensure that all the available resources are utilized to maximize the effectiveness of these programs (DuFour, 2008).

Accountability

In reviewing and sharing the information gathered in PGPs, leaders would be able to plan for and work on areas that appear to be weak as well as maintain strength. Understanding data and sharing the results with parents will give a better understanding of performance and assure them that the staff is working on maintaining or improving crime rates. Sharing results also helps to build community relations and trust (Loertscher, 2005). Leaders should be prepared for eventualities; ensuring expectations for themselves and their staff by encouraging them to live up to the expectations of their job. Support mental sharing and learning from one another (Sajeva, 2007). Planning for developing predictive gang prevention programs and identifying needs and providing for them are some of the ways of ensuring success. Thigpen (2011) emphasized that criminal justice leaders should have "knowledge to reform" as well as the "knowledge of the dynamics of change" (p. 2). This knowledge is likely to help these leaders effectively implement and maintain PGP (Thigpen, 2011).

Criminal Justice Organizations

PGPs are implemented at all levels of the criminal justice system (Hodges, 2003). The underlining components of PGPs in all these criminal justice institutions are collaboration and achievement (Hughes-Hassell, Brasfield, & Dupree, 2012). At each level PGP may appear different depending on the organization (Spanneut, 2010). As they prepare to face the challenges that come with entering the profession for the first time, new gang investigators can benefit from participating in predictive gang prevention programs as they can learn from more experienced gang investigators in their community (Lovett & Cameron, 2011).

Predictive Gang Prevention Programs

A PGP is a collaborative team or group that consists of members who "work together, interdependently" toward common goals and purposes of learning (DuFour, DuFour, & Eaker, 2008, p. 469). Each member of the group is mutually accountable for the success or failure of the group. During the initial phases of PGPs, studies showed that efforts were meagerly supported by the majority and/or the versions of PGP implemented lacked depth and quality (Dufour, 2008). Erkens and Talbert (2012) posited that effective leaders are those who have a thorough understanding of their requirements and how to carry them out.

Components

The components of PGP include: team building, professional development, knowledge, communication, setting goals, and deliberate planning for improvement (Dufour, 2008). Each member in PGP has their own function and understanding these roles is critical to the effective function of PGP. In many ways, PGPs are run by leaders who take a hands-off approach; to address this, Costa (2013) stressed the need for leaders to be "visible, accessible, and taking time out to meet" (p. 97). Lovett et al., (2011) stated administrators such as principles are responsible for defining the purpose and establishing the goals that will help first-time gang investigators become successful. In PGP the focus is on sharing, collaborating, knowledge management, and team work rather than the assertion of power. According to Sajeva (2007), knowledge management barriers are addressed by giving every employee a mission to transform the perception that "information is power" into the perception that "information sharing is power" (p. 26). PGP can be used to achieve this power through team building and collaborating with fellow leaders to discuss concepts that are mutually beneficial (Sajeva, 2007). Costa (2013) posited that due to a highly aging staff and turnover levels, there is significant inconsistencies in PGPs. For PGP to work, improving, gaining, imparting, and managing knowledge in the current criminal justice system needs to be emphasized by criminal justice leaders (Costa, 2013).

Characteristics

PGPs are characterized by a collaborative culture, inquiry, common mission, vision communication, and collective goals. Jones, Stall, and Yarbrough (2013) stated that in effective PGPs there is an alignment of goals with vision for the future. These goals should be clearly stated and communicated to stakeholders, there should be a collaborative effort institution wide and not just selected areas (Loertscher, 2008b). PGP should reflect evidence of student learning, AYP, and educator performance. In Bailey's (2014) study, the participants revealed that PGP not only improved performance but it improved the culture. Implementing PGP as a means of promoting collaboration is a difficult task, but the results can be very rewarding (Bailey, 2014). Bailey emphasized that although PGPs are effective, there are many challenges to effectively "sustain" them, due to time constraints and conflicts of priorities (p. 3). Thigpen concluded that implementing a professional learning community requires the combined efforts of administrators and other stake holders to "navigate technical and adaptive challenges" (Thigpen, 2011, p. 75).

Misconceptions

Current misconceptions of PGP include the notion that having PGPs always yields success (Bailey, 2014). Using the term PGP loosely by itself will not translate to a successful criminal justice system (Loertscher, 2005). Setting realistic goals and planning effectively for improvement is critical to the survival of PGPs (Jones et al., 2013). Schechter (2012) postulated that if leaders and educators tackle their fear and eliminate collaborative barriers PGPs will not be just another theoretical fad.

Collaboration

A culture of collaboration is essential to the growth and development of criminal justice organizations. Bailey (2014) found that predictive gang prevention programs (PGP) are essential in the collaborative process, even for educators who have many years of service. Criminal justice leaders create an environment in which participatory leadership flourishes and employees feel valued, motivated, and believe in self-improvement while improving the organization (Parker, 2008). Boundaries are eliminated and members engage in partnerships with organizational leaders who have specific expertise that is used to provide impeccable results. According to Bailey (2014), seasoned teachers find the experience of participating in PGP as rewarding and helpful to their practice. In a successful PGP, members collaborate, plan, assign tasks, assign roles, and monitor programs (Erkens & Talbert, 2012). This allows leaders to address employee development and evaluate team strategy while finalizing assigned projects.

Team Building in PGPs

The specific purpose of a PGP team is established and clarified in concert with the institution's vision and mission statement (Hoffman, 2003). In the goal setting process each member of the team gets the opportunity to participate and ensure measurability of these goals. Each goal is clarified and communicated to members in comprehensible language. This helps to guarantee lucidity and relevance to the tasks for which the goals are being developed. PGPs are self-managed teams; the emphasis is not on power and structure but on collaboration and collaborative inquiry (Erkens & Talbert, 2012). In Thompson's (2008) 'Making the Team' text; the author highlighted that emphasis should be placed on self-management teams which reduces member power. Strategic design of a team effectively exemplifies an organization's mission, vision, value, content, and strategy (Hoffman, 2003). It involves selecting the finest individuals that exhibit the best quality that will be consistent with the institution's philosophy and success (Thompson, 2008).

In PGPs, teams should be formed for a specific specialized task and it is imperative to include individuals with experience that will contribute to the team in the best manner. Establishing a team is important but strategically designing the team requires critical thinking, a clear purpose, focus on environment, the structure of the team, diversity, timelines, and goal alignment (Yuki, 2010). To ensure continued success innovativeness is crucial; innovation should be a team norm in criminal justice institutions and it is reinforced by the organizational culture with a strong belief in becoming more advanced at facilitating cultural transformation (Smith, 2012). Each team member promotes and utilizes critical thinking, motivates others, collaborates with others, applies theory to practice, and applies self-evaluation techniques (Dufour, 2010). By using these strategies team leaders address competitive, persistent, emotional intelligence, and effectiveness of the team (Mayer, Salovey, & Caruso, 2008).

Sustainability of PGPs

Sustainability is central to the survival of PGPs criminal justice organization; strategies for sustainability include effective planning, innovation, employee retention, evaluation of PGPs continuous assessment, and a culture of adaptability (Mullen & Schunk, 2010). A leader can create a culture of adaptability in PGP by modeling desirable, innovative actions, and motivating employees to become leaders (Maital & Seshadri, 2007). Great leaders ensure that there are opportunities for promotion or increased incentives for their hard work. Leaders should promote a collaborative culture in which they delegate responsibilities, provide training opportunities, and include subordinates in the decision-making process (Rismark & Solvberg, 2011). It is also essential that PGP members understand issues and make provisions to minimize the impact of these issues. According to Teague and Anfara (2012), understanding that each day comes with new challenges of sustaining new programs; collaborating with team members, and ensuring flexibility always aides in improving the organization.

Innovation

According to AbuJarad et al. (2010), innovation involves "coming up with new ideas" and incorporating them into new and established processes (p. 309). Smith (2012) noted that, "Innovation is a social phenomenon that not only requires many people to generate and implement ideas, but also requires that those individuals interact, work together, and build on one another's perspectives, thinking, and creativity" (p. 3). Hickman (2010) emphasized the notion that effective leadership is necessary for professional growth. It is important for leaders to develop knowledgeable workers, help to build their skills, and value employees expertise. Great leaders are not seen a bosses but individuals who are focused on the best interest of the organization and those who build it (Maital & Seshadri, 2007). Innovation in PGPs involves the implementation of mentorship programs for new teachers; it involves ongoing professional development for new and veteran educators (Bailey, 2014).

The Importance of Data

It is difficult to be an effective leader of an organization if decisions are largely dependent on data collected from previous years. Criminal justice institutions are organizations that impact the lives of practically everyone at some point or another. Hodges (2003) stated that the impact can be even greater if the results from a comprehensive analysis of data from previous programs are used to improve the lives of the children we encounter each year. In PGPs criminal justice leaders and other educators need to understand that data is important (Hoffman, 2003). Some of the types of information that would help leaders to make effective decisions in PGPs are: ethnicity, economical status of students, public opinion polls, and attendance.

Data should be used to tell a story of performance. Dufour et al. (2008) emphasized the importance to share the success of the achievement with the community. Using data to help build community relations as well as provide clarity for PGP members is recommended. This would create a kind of open or limited forum in which stakeholders will feel valued, knowing that they are given access to information and through explanation (Hoffman, 2003). An additional benefit of using data in PGP is securing community support, especially in areas such as fund raising, donations, and volunteerism. Parents and other stakeholders tend to be excited to share in the success of their students and are ready and willing to offer solutions in areas that need improvements (Jones et al., 2013).

An effective leader should use data to increase students' performance through modification and strengthening of existing PGPs while creating new programs (Lovett et al., 2011). The collection of data can help leaders to do a thorough assessment of programs, to see what does and what does not work. This will help to reduce the cost of funding unnecessary and ineffective programs, thus reserving money to be allocated to those programs that are useful (Costa, 2013). Using data to assess programs also aides in determining the areas of instructions that are weak and those that are strong. In doing this, decisions can be made about the amount of time that is allotted to specific areas of instruction. During PGP meetings, data collection is imperative in identifying which standards are being met and those that require more focus (Jay, Karen, Cockrell, & Valentine, 1999).

Hollingsworth (2012) posited that the allocation of resources for PGPs is also dependent on data. Specific departments and areas of instruction may require more resources than others. According to Darling-Hammond (2006), it is therefore important to collect information from these departments and to choose where to distribute the resources. Other factors bearing on the gathering and analysis of data are: appointment, placement, rotation, and training of staff (Hughes-Hassell et al., 2012). Once new programs have been in place, there might be a need to appoint new staff members and provide training for them as well the existing ones (Chow, 2013). This will improve staff performance and efficiency in administering these new programs as well as the required tools to analyze their effectiveness.

Using data is important; however, administrators should ensure that leadership and monitoring of new programs brought about by the use of data is visibly supported (Riveros, 2012). There should be commitment to the use of effort and action in order to make these programs work. Data collection should be an ongoing, formative process, which should be used on a regular basis and throughout as a whole (Darling-Hammond, 2006). The data should not scare or overwhelm staff members, but be presented in a disaggregated manner which makes it easier to understand. It is imperative to hold ongoing meetings to explain the purpose of the data collected and the most effective use of this data to create successful PGP through improved planning for students' achievement (Hughes-Hassell et al., 2012).

Communication

According to Ales, Rodrigues, Snyder, and Conklin (2011), an effective component to acquiring a successful collaborative team is communication. PGP requires openness, effective communication, and encouragement from team members (Ales et al., 2011). Gadeken (2012) states that instructional leader should focus consistently on "recruiting, developing, and maintaining team members." Consistent communication and sharing knowledge is essential to a collaborative success in s (p. 44). For leaders to overcome the many barriers associated with acquiring knowledge is to make followers aware of and develop the urge to transform the notion "information is power" to "Information sharing is power" (Sajeva, 2007, p. 26).

Ethical Consideration

Criminal justice leaders can reshape an unethical organizational culture by being role models for employees in PGPs (Costa, 2013). It is important that leaders practice what they preach by instilling the correct values in employees and ensuring that their actions are ethical as well. Burgess, Newton, and Riveros (2012) posited that constant communication between leaders and employees is crucial; leaders need to remind employees of ethical principles through memos, newsletters, bulletins, and other media. According to Donaldson (1992) there should be constant professional development activities and refresher courses regarding "code of ethics, code of conduct, sexual discrimination/harassment, human welfare, rights, duties, responsibilities, and social contracts" that are made available and in most cases mandatory for employees to participate in.

According to Jones (2010), unethical behavior occurs as a result of self-interest. It is therefore crucial for organizations to focus on the employees' interest collectively. Transformational leaders encourage open, honest, and timely communication, and foster dialogue and collaboration between team members (Amar, Hentrich, & Hlupic, 2009). In transforming an organization, leaders need to also transform the culture of the organization; this may require modification to the organization's vision and mission to incorporate the ethical principles that will improve the organization (Jones, 2010). There should also be a system of reward for upholding ethical behaviors and consequences for breaking them. An example of a reward could be verbal or written recognition for departments that consistently uphold the ethical culture of keeping students' data confidential and promoting ethical principles.

Motivational Interviewing

Cassondra Flanagan was present for an in-depth presentation by Bob Brzenchek, and intrigued by the level of detail and sophistication of gang activity. Cassondra Flanagan personally spent 8 years in the United States Army, having joined at 17 years old. Her first duty station was Camp Casey, Korea. She was thrilled to be a part of the after-hours fun that came with life as a female soldier. Balancing responsibility with social expectations and late nights at the club was a norm. In the military, this balancing act serves as a rite of passage into adulthood. Unfortunately, gang violence amongst young soldiers from all parts of the United States was also a norm. There were the Philippians from California, and the Samoans from Hawaii. There were the African-American Bloods from cities on the east coast, and the African-American "grey and black" gangs from Chicago and New York. There were white skinheads from the south, and the white radical Christians also from the south. The types were endless. Based on rank and file, one could be easily promoted or demoted, in uniform; and or raped, maimed, or stabbed at a club along converging territorial lines outside of uniform. While stationed at Camp Casey, Korea, many such altercations took place outside of uniform. More often than not soldiers would fight each other at bars based on supposed disrespect of regional gang affiliation. In the spirit of comradery and service to the community Cassondra saw fit to suggest a preventative solution to Bob, and anyone reading this passage. Per Ronald Reagan, let's make America great again! Cassondra strongly believes Motivational Interviewing is a pivotal and innovative technique capable of deterring gang membership early on. Likely, a vital piece to transforming America and bringing positive change to our nation's safety and thwarting the current addiction crisis. Per Bob's presentation and a little extra homework, she learned that disenfranchised American youth are more likely to join gangs. The gang initiation process includes a level of mental and physical manipulations that generally stunts the initiate's ability to make sound decisions absent of an O.G.'s approval. Motivational Interviewing is designed to assist anyone in making clear choices and resolving any crippling double-sided thoughts.

Perhaps it's best to go into a specific detail about the scope and range of Motivational Interviewing. Let's review some general insight into the history and origin of this counseling technique. Then begin a brief explanation of various methods of implementation, noting throughout what programs have seen measurable positive results with the techniques, as well as interjecting a relative example of how Motivational Interviewing has been a successful tool in aiding veterans in varying degrees of crisis. Finally, lets discus how and why Motivational Interviewing will be a useful tool in curtailing gang recruitment and or convincing young members to espouse their gang affiliation and put down their flags.

Motivational Interviewing (MI) was initially developed by William R. Miller in 1983. According to its developers, Miller and Rollnick, 'Motivational interviewing is a way of being with a client, not just a set of techniques for doing counseling'. It is a unified style of communication in which the person being interviewed becomes the sole focus and emphasizes eliciting and one's strengthening motivation to change.

The motivational processes within the individual are the driving force. The ultimate focus of MI is on exploring and resolving ambivalence. Well-sited research from the 1960's proves that what people say both internally and externally is directly reflected in their belief about themselves and the way they interact within society. In other words, getting people to open up and talk is a golden opportunity to allow an individual to initiate change. In other words, in order to know what you want to change and why you want to change it; you first have to hear yourself say what you are doing and experiencing out loud. Individuals considering joining a gang could benefit from hearing what gang recruiters are telling them. Something will awaken in their own awareness if they repeat slowly the brainwashing techniques presented to them, instead of silently listening in agreement.

Through clinical experience and empirical research, the fundamental principles of MI have been applied and tested in an array of settings and for a exorbitant array of purposes. Yet, never specifically applied to gang prevention, MI is a well-established counseling solution effectively encouraging people to change addictive behavior in adolescents as well as adults. Proven to deter everything from substance abuse to spousal abuse, it has also proven effective in parental and marital counseling, counseling within juvenile detentions centers, adult transitioning, and prison re-entry programs, as well as other areas within the scope of social work where an individual is experiencing or expressing ambivalence. While relatively few studies have examined MI's effectiveness in reducing risky behaviors such as engaging in unprotected sex or sharing needles, the meta-analysis of the technique from studies conducted between 1998 and 2003 reveals strong positive outcomes in favor of MI over varying forms of group therapy and comparable inpatient psycho-therapeutic alternatives. With respect to gangs, per Bob Brzenchek, young people in the U.S. are joining at alarming rates. Young people could certainly benefit from what MI has to offer. Not only is it an evidence-based, statistically proven useful tool for cancelling ambivalent thoughts, MI may serve as a lifelong coping mechanism for disparaged youth to lean on when facing difficult decisions in the future.

Any MI practitioner must be well trained at identifying ambivalence and the five principals of MI according to Miller and Rollnick. Here is how a practitioner would go about identifying ambivalence, including personal accounts, and interspersing specific methods. Ambivalence, by definition, is the state of having mixed feelings or contradictory ideas about something or someone. Ambivalence causes a level of uncertainty even amongst healthy individuals. Depending on the severity, however, it has the capacity to paralyze an individual, rendering them incapable of making a choice. The effect is unhealthy. As a Case Manager (CM), for a veterans housing program Cassondra had the privilege of counseling many veterans expressing a state of desperation. Note, desperation is a red flag counselors look for because it points to a level of ambivalence. Let's look at a former housing program participant. We'll call him D.D. He suffered from drug addiction and homelessness. The program he participated in had a specific goal of placing homeless veterans in housing within a 90-day window. It operated with a "housing first" model. Program designated as housing first models believed that solving a homeless problem will inevitably solve all other issues participants face. Therefore, staff within these programs only focused on housing. A clear picture of daily tasks was more along the lines of realtor advocating for heroic citizens with little to no income.

As part of the initial plan of action, Cassondra spent a week ushering D.D. to a number of apartment buildings and rooming houses throughout the city of Philadelphia. Every option presented to D.D. was fantastic and appeared move-in ready, per his standards and commentary. At our daily closing remarks D.D. would say, "Miss Flanagan you're too picky. I loves this place. Let's sign the paperwork. You're giving these guys [meaning the property owners] too much of a hassle." In response, Cassondra Flanagan reminded him of the plan he agreed to, and they would make a choice to peruse a specific location at the end of the week. She did this because she had higher expectations of what he deserved and what the program should offer him. Nearly all of the standard habitations available accepting tenants with D.D.'s criminal history were deplorable. Philadelphia is not a forgiving place when it comes to real estate. (Note: my response was not necessarily in keeping with the guidelines of Motivational Interviewing, rather the goal and scope of the programs standard operating procedure. The program did eventually begin training staffers on MI. However, the emphasis here is on desperation as an indicator of ambivalence). Before the weeks' end D.D. confided in me that he owed some people money where he was "living" and he needed to get out of there as soon as possible. She told him owing money was not a crime and it takes a while for someone to file proceedings against him to recoup moneys owed and have their day in court. D.D. began crying. He stated that he and his girlfriend were addicted to crack cocaine and that he sent her into hiding with his family in the suburbs. But the dealers, "young boys," as he referred to them, were wild and have killed several people in the neighborhood. Through conversation she learned D.D. did not and would not under any circumstance file a police report. He also did not want to move outside of the city because he feared he wouldn't have access to crack cocaine. Furthermore, D.D. explained that he knew the drug was bad for him. But, his girlfriend was also important to him and he would only try quitting if she did. "I can't bear to leave her in these streets without me," he said. Cassondra successfully placed D.D. into housing within the time-frame given, per program guidelines, case closed. Cassondra maintained professional contact with D.D. via joint veteran networks and housing initiatives. She watched D.D. ping-pong through various veteran direct service programs during that time. Some of those networks were drug treatment programs, others were housing specific. In conversation and in confidence D.D. would inform her that he was only in yet another program to seek refuge from the "young boys." One memorable day D.D. sought Cassondra out in confidence to detail the night his girlfriend died by his side in an abandoned building, due to a drug overdose. "Miss Flanagan it's not worth it, the drugs. It's not worth it. Can you call someone so I can get clean. I just didn't want to leave her. But, she left me," he said. She arranged for D.D.'s acceptance into an inpatient treatment program. After which, he entered a recovery housing program, and has been successfully clean and sober (over 2 years to date).

As previously mentioned, an energy of desperation and lack of motivation are the hallmarks of someone crippled by ambivalence. Disenfranchised gang recruits join gangs out of desperation. Desperation due to uncertain housing circumstance and access to drugs, or desperation due to loneliness and fear of acceptance is all the same with regards to the way one's psyche is affected. MI's developers observed that desperation is not an indicator of readiness or willingness to change, rather a natural reaction. Therefore, anyone drawing upon the basic skills and techniques of MI should not infer that an individual in this state is expressing denial or resistance. It would have been easy to assume D.D. was only using his girlfriend as an excuse. Such a faulty inference will undoubtedly result in unnecessary discord, damaging the counselor participant relationship. Every person/participant picks up on the subtleties of judgmental behavior. Especially those people living on the margins of society. Gang recruits tend to live on the margins of society and they have romanticized what living a marginal life is like. MI is designed to utilize an individual's intrinsic nature to circumvent factors traditionally viewed by field experts as roadblocks to listening. Those roadblocks are listed by Thomas Gordon, Ph.D. as: giving advice, making suggestions, providing solutions, persuading with logic, arguing, lecturing, moralizing, preaching, disagreeing, judging, criticizing and/or blaming, shaming, ridiculing and/or labeling, interpreting and/or analyzing, reassuring, sympathizing and or consoling, questioning and or probing, withdrawing, distracting and or humoring. Essentially, hallmarks of judgmental inferences.

The housing first program of which Cassondra Flanagan was employed to house D.D. began implementing two important techniques specific to MI. Both have already proven to be indispensable tools for social workers (SW) and CM's to use to further assist program participants in accomplishing their housing goals. She had the honorable task of lecturing her colleagues on such techniques. Both are acronyms', the first one is Desire, Ability, Reason and Need (DARN), and the other Critical Time Intervention (CTI). Both of these techniques require detailed fundamental understanding of basic skills and principals of MI. Those skills are defined by the acronym O.A.R.S. (Open-ended questions. Affirmations. Reflective listening. Summarizing statements) and yet another acronym representing principals is D.E.A.R.S. (Develop discrepancy. Express empathy. Amplify ambivalence. Support self-efficacy) respectively. Let's detail these unique skills and principals as we move forward.

DARN is designed to bring hyper awareness, elevating the counselor's listening skills so one may take advantage of the very personal and self-reflective verbal ques a client gives. DARN are best understood to be the prerequisite for commitment. DARN requires that the counselor elicit client motivation through what is referred to as "change talk." DARN comments express a reason for change. Keep in mind that is not the same thing as agreeing to change. They are the, in passe, verbiage participant's use that may serve as ques that they are considering changing a behavior. When conversing with a participant, it is important to identify and encourage change talk. One reason MI is described as client-centered is because change talk usually contains intimate individual reasons for change that hold a particular importance unique to the individual being counseled. When an individual is prepared to change, his own brand of change talk will serve as the blueprint of the actual change process. Change talk is best used to address discrepancies between word and deed. A skilled counselor will highlight the contradiction between what gangs promise youth and what they actually provide. Protection, family, and identity versus danger, isolation, and loss of self-identity. Desire is the kind of change talk that expresses a preference for change. The client gives verbal cues suggesting an affinity towards changing the status quo. In the case of D.D. frequent crack cocaine use and constantly running from dealers and hiding his girlfriend was the status quo. A good MI practitioner would encourage him to talk more about how unnerving such a lifestyle is. Honing in on a participant's statements relating to personal capacity assists a counselor with encouraging ability. Perhaps a gang member would describe how they could move out of town or hide until the gang stops seeking them out. D.D. clearly stated that he could not recover from crack cocaine unless his girlfriend was also willing to recover, not a strong sense of independent ability there. So, an MI practitioner should attempt to steer the conversation away from such talk. Reasons often occurs in conjunction with desire. Yet, reasons should be heard and identified separately. Ambivalence causes a client to fluctuate in either desire to change and or reason for changing a specific behavior depending on mood. D.D. didn't like always fleeing from dangerous drug dealers. Similar situations occur with gang initiates. D.D. also couldn't stand the thought of leaving his girlfriend. The divide in his mind is what caused his ambivalence and ultimately kept him in a state of desperation. It's a deadlock on the mind, where a person is reluctant to make a choice. In similar vein, many female gang participants and affiliates site being closer to their boyfriend as the impetus for staying in the gang. By distinguishing between reason and desire a counselor becomes fluid in hearing and effectively re-directing the client towards change. Need is best identified by statements of obligation. D.D. felt the need to protect is girlfriend. In other situations, need is a positive indicator of change talk, perhaps a parent may feel the need to get clean in order to provide for their children. A gang member may need the gang's muscle to continue selling the drugs, whose money he relies on to live. Each case and client will differ. The message history and personal experience is that D.A.R.N. plays an important role in helping counselors flesh out and encourage participants to say things to themselves that facilitate change and resolve ambivalence. Again, in order to know what you want to change and why you want to change it; you first have to hear yourself say what you are doing and experiencing out loud. Critical Time Intervention (CTI) worked well with the veterans housing program D.D. was enrolled in because the program emphasized a 90-day window or less. As the name suggests, CTI is provided at a critical time. A time when an individual is feeling the effects of ambivalent behavior the most. Perhaps if and when a school notices changes in a student seemingly gang induced. Education professionals could intervene and suggest and or require a short-term program utilizing the techniques of MI and CTI collectively to help students make better life choices, provide them with new ways of coping, and avoid gang membership. Research shows that if ambivalence is not resolved the individual will accept whatever is presented without decisively choosing. Therefore, the critical time is when young gang recruits are at an impasse. CTI is most useful when an individual must make definitive choices that may forever alter the trajectory of their life. Typically during transition from an institutional setting to a community setting, for example, local shelter to independent living or elementary school to middle schoo. The goal is to facilitate smooth transition by strengthening a participant's ties to informal and formal community supports. Teaching clients to prioritize decision making based on logic and rational options. Utilizing CTI and MI to collectively to counsel D.D., would have encouraged him to explor his safety in relation to his girlfriend and juxtapose to his and her health in more detail. Perhaps he would have decided to prioritize the situation differently.

O.A.R.S. is the skill set required to make this interviewing technique possible. MI practitioners must be in the habit of formulating open-ended questions like, "What happens when you behave that way?" and "What's that like for you?" offer the client the option of expressing his or her thoughts freely. These questions also make communicative space for the counselor to exercise Reflective listening and Summary statements. When reflective listening is done right a counselor builds empathy with clients. Reflective listening involves mirroring the individual's body language and paraphrasing their response. The practice of reflective listening serves two functions: it insures that the counselor properly understood what was said and it deepens the conversation by allowing the participant to hear again what they said, and in turn, understand their own thoughts better. Summarizing statements perform as a similar function to reflective listening, but can be a major help in developing discrepancy, often what is said discretely is not what is meant precisely. Summarizing also allows the counselor to transition to the next topic by pulling together everything stated. "Let me see if I understand you correctly," and "Here's what I heard. Tell me if I missed something," constitute good examples of summarizing statements. Counselors should also make a point to utilize Affirming responses especially when a participant expresses a level of vulnerability during conversation. "I've really enjoyed our discussion today" and "you've tried very hard to quit" are excellent examples of affirming responses.

Cassondra Flanagan sincerely desires that the reader finish this excerpt with a clear conceptualization of what MI entails and how it may be beneficial in our nation's quest to rid our neighborhood's inner city, suburban, or otherwise of drugs and violence. Cassondra doesn't proclaim to know all there is to know about gangs, nor is she is a clinical psychologist. However, she is a subject matter expert with degrees in Forensic Science and Anthropology. Her exorbitant experience utilizing Motivational Interviewing while counseling marginalized cliental, convinced her that this is an effective technique. Moreover, it is the perfect prevention counseling method for any gang prevention program.

16 Findings

According to the OJJDP, parents play an important role in keeping young people out of gangs. There are many things parents can do to help their children stay away from gangs, including monitoring their activities, fostering close relationships with them, and using positive and consistent discipline. However, parents often lack factual information about gangs. This guide is designed to provide parents with answers to common questions about gangs to enable them to recognize and prevent gang involvement. There are a lot of reasons why youth get involved in gangs. Sometimes youth get "pulled" into a gang because they think they might earn a lot of money and gain status, or they may think it is a good way to show family, neighborhood, or cultural pride. Other times youth get "pushed" into a gang because they are afraid for their safety and think a gang will provide protection from neighborhood crime and violence, or they have been pressured by the gang to join. Even though some youth believe that gang involvement might provide safety, protection, excitement, and opportunities to earn money, the truth is that gang involvement is very dangerous and limits opportunities for the future. Research has shown that youth who are gang-involved are more likely to commit crimes, which increases their chances of being arrested and incarcerated, and to be victims of violence themselves. Young girls are especially vulnerable to sexual victimization. Youth who get caught up in gangs are also less likely to graduate high school, less likely to find stable jobs, and more likely to have alcohol and drug problems and even health problems later in life. The most common age that youth join a gang is around 15, but the early adolescent years (12–14 years of age) are a crucial time when youth are exposed to gangs and may consider joining a gang. While it is more common for boys to get involved in gangs, girls also face similar pushes and pulls and can also become involved in gangs. Gang involvement can be fluid, as some youth move in and out of gang-involved friendship groups. Thus, parents should pay attention to even small changes in behavior.

Recommendations

According to the OJJDP, "talk to your child about the negative consequences of gang behaviors and ways to avoid them. Be clear that you disapprove of gangs and do not want to see your child hurt or arrested. Be firm in your expectations that your child should NOT: Associate with any gang-involved individuals. Hang out where gang members congregate. Attend any party or social event sponsored by gangs. Use any kind of hand or finger signs that may be meaningful to gangs, especially in pictures (even as a joke). Wear clothing that may have meaning to gangs in your area (explain to your child that these clothing items can put him or her in danger and that you will not purchase them or allow them to be worn)" (2016).

According to the *Public Safety Geography, A Quarterly Bulletin of Applied Geography for the Study of Crime & Public Safety*, as law enforcement agencies have adopted computerized records management systems and geographic information systems, their ability to assemble and analyze data about crime and disorder has soared. Widely available large data sets and new analytical tools are transforming policing. Our technological capabilities have grown faster than our capacity to understand and react to the ethical implications of these new capabilities. As place based policing, hot spot policing, intelligence-led policing, and information-based policing merge into the science and practice of predictive policing, police will confront increasingly complex ethical issues. An excellent example of these issues concerns the relationship between income, housing, and crime. While the literature long ago established the nexus between poverty, substandard housing, and crime, geocoded crime data now allow police to visualize the relationship more clearly, and provides information so that the police can better deploy resources and target crime. Moreover, predictive policing principles suggest that given known factors, we can predict those areas where crime and disorder are likely to emerge (Volume 2 Issue 4|March 2011).

Conclusion

The gang mentality is strongly correlative with the socialization phenomenon inherent in the human species. My personal thoughts on this are that we are naturally social creatures who gravitate toward assimilating into groups that give us meaning within the confines of our contexts. The gang phenomenon is also strongly associated with socio-economic, cultural, and familial factors which leads me to believe the influence on gang formation is largely a product of the underlying social woes of that society. In the case of America in relation to the world, it seems that this will get presumably worse than better given the geopolitical shifting going on in the world at present.

Assuming that collaboration through the implementation of effective, organized gang prevention programs there can be improvement at all levels of the criminal justice system. In addition, leaders who plan more effectively by strategically sharing knowledge and strategies will improve performance. To arrive at a logical conclusion and be able to make recommendations regarding these effects, and the impact the strategy may have on leaders and other key stakeholders who are invested are likely to succeed.

Following the determination of the differences and best practices to see if there have been any major differences in crime rates, the extent to which the performance and overall improvement will be realized. The basis of these assumptions came when Brzenchek was a police officer in the District of Columbia. Gang prevention programs were being introduced and many criminal justice leaders were tasked to implement the program. There was a complete hands-off approach by the leaders and police officers were a bit bewildered with the program and what was expected.

The sociological perspective emphasizes the role of socialization as a prime factor in shaping behavior. "Socialization is a process of social development and learning that occurs as individuals interact with one another and learn about society's expectations for acceptable behavior", according to Delaney (2014a). In taking a hard line with self-accountability and placing blame squarely on the shoulders of the narcotics abusers with vigilance on both law enforcement's part and NEPA, citizens all hinder the financing of gangs and other criminal activities threatening society, which is channeled by demand of the narcotics trade. The fallout from the illegal abuse of power and illegitimate monetary flows from the illegal narcotics trade, legalization is not the answer. Even in a heavily regulated narcotics trade, society as a whole would revert to the turn of the century where domestic and international implications would be heightened narcotics abuse, profiteering, deteriorating societal health, and a broken public relief system.

Afterword

We wrote this book to examine the criminal gangster mindset and offer perspectives on predictive gang prevention strategies. The real-world examples provided demonstrated a holistic approach towards combatting this surging societal problem. It outlined the evolution of gang membership: from a state of interest, to association, to hardcore, "O.G." (Original Gangster) status. Credence was given to the role—and importance—of the immediate family of the gang member, whether they are supportive of the member's activities or vehemently opposed to it. Case studies augmented by examples of how law enforcement has evolved from creating Gang Units and Violent Crime Task Forces, documenting and tracking of gang activity were outlined. The authors explained how law enforcement has used and continues to use a multi-pronged approach in combating criminal street gang violence today which has morphed from the arrest and release mentality of the 1970s and 1980s to partnering with private organizations such as the Boys & Girls Clubs. In-depth profiles, with lengthy histories of the gang member subjects and their transformations, were provided to demonstrate how hardcore gang members are a menace to society.

References

AbuJarad, et.al (2010). Innovation Creation and Innovation Adoption: A approaches (3rd ed.). Thousand Oaks, CA: Sage.

Ahmed, M. (2010). Criminal justice as transformation – criminal justice for transformation. *Development*, 53(4), 511–517. doi:10.1057/dev.2010.70.

Ales, M. W., Rodrigues, S.B., Snyder, R., & Conklin, M. (2011, Fall). Developing and implementing an effective framework for collaboration: The experience of the CS2day collaborative, Journal of Continuing Education in the Health, Professions, 31(1), S12–S20.

Amar, A. D., Hentrich, C., & Hlupic, V. (2009). To be a better leader, give up authority. *Harvard Business Review*, 87(12), 22–24.

Anderson, 2000; McDonald, 2003; Mendoza-Denton, 2008, Code of the Street: Decency, Violence, and the Moral Life of the Inner City. New York: W.W. Norton & Company.

Avila, J. (2009). Predictive gang prevention programs. *Language Arts*, 86(4), 312–313. Retrieved from http://search.proquest.com/docview/196839152?accountid=35812.

Avolio, B. J., & Yammarino, F. J. (2002). *Transformational and charismatic leadership: The road ahead.* San Diego, CA: Emerald.

Barber, 1993; Beyer, 1994; Klein, 1995; Quinn & Downs, 1993; Spergel et al., 1990; Zevitz & Takata, 1992, Anatomy of a Gang Suppression Unit: The Social Construction of an Organizational Response to Gangs, First Published September 7, 2012 Research Article Police Quarterly, 06/1999, Volume 2, Issue 2

Birr, S. (2016, March 25). MS-13 gang recruiting young illegal immigrants, fueling crime in DC. *The Daily Caller*. Retrieved from http://dailycaller.com/2016/03/25/ms-13-gang-recruiting-young-illegal-immigrants-fueling-crime-in-dc/.

Brotherton, D. C. (2004). *The almighty latin king and queen nation: Street politics and the transformation of a New York City gang.* New York: Columbia University Press.

Burgess, D., Newton, P., & Riveros, A. (2012). A situated account of teacher agency and learning: critical reflections on predictive gang prevention programs. *Canadian Journal of Criminal Justice*, 35(1), 202.

Chow, A. (2013). Predictive gang prevention programs in three subject departments in Hong Kong secondary schools. *International Journal of Arts & Sciences*, 6(4), 233–245. Retrieved from http://search.proquest.com/docview/1496696409?accountid=35812.

Christensen, L. B., Johnson, R. B., & Turner, L. A. (2011). *Research methods, design, and analysis* (6th ed.). Boston, MA: Allyn & Bacon.

Cilesiz, S. (2011). A phenomenological approach to experiences with technology: current state, promise, and future directions for research. *Criminal Justiceal Technology Research & Development*, 59(4), 487–510. doi:10.1007/s11423-010-9173-2.

Commission, N. J. (2015, 12 01). Gangs of New York and how close you live to them. *NY Daily News*. Retrieved from http://interactive.nydailynews.com/2015/12/gangs-of-new-york-city-interactive-map/.

Costa, S. D. (2013). *Leadership in the barrington public school professional learning community*. (Order No. 3596391, Northeastern University). *ProQuest Dissertations and Theses*, 185. Retrieved from http://search.proquest.com/docview/1448275160?accountid=35812. (1448275160).

Creswell, J. W. (2013). *Qualitative inquiry & research design: Choosing among five approaches* (3rd ed.). Thousand Oaks, CA: Sage.

Creswell, J. W. (2014). *Qualitative inquiry & research design: Choosing among five approaches* (4th ed.). Thousand Oaks, CA: Sage.

Dance, 2002; Flores-Gonzalez, 2002, Tough Fronts: The Impact of Street Culture on Schooling. New York: Routledge.

Darling-Hammond, L. (2006). No child left behind and high reform. *Harvard Criminal Justice Review*, 76(4), 642–667, 725. Retrieved from http://search.proquest.com/docview/212299060?accountid=35812.

Delaney, R. (2014). The price of prisons: What incarceration costs taxpayers? Federal Sentencing Reporter, 25(1), 68–80.

Domash, S. F. (1999, May 1). Working gangs from inside prison. *Police Magazine*. Retrieved from www.policemag.com/channel/gangs/articles/1999/05/model-corrections-programs-works-successfully-with-police-to-gang-up-on-crimes.aspx.

Donaldson, T. (1992). The language of international corporate ethics. *Business Ethics Quarterly*, 2(3), 271–281.

DuFour, R., DuFour, R., & Eaker, R. (2008). Revisiting predictive gang prevention programs at work: new insights for improving schools. *Teacher Librarian*, 37(4), 75. Retrieved from http://search.proquest.com/docview/224871692?accountid=35812.

DuFour, R., DuFour, R., Eaker, R., & Many, T. (2010). *Learning by doing: A handbook for predictive gang prevention programs at work* (2nd ed.). Bloomington, IN: Solution Tree Press.

Dunn, J. (1999). *Los Angeles crips and bloods: Past and present*. Palo Alto, CA: EDGE (Ethics in Development in a Global Environment), Stanford University.

"Enhancing Motivation for Change in Substance Abuse Treatment". Treatment Improvement Protocol (TIP 35). SAMHSA (2002). USDHHS: Rockville, MD.

Erkens, C., & Twadell, E. (2012). *Leading by design: An action framework for PGP at Work™ leaders*. Bloomington, IN: Solution Tree Press.

Esquibel, K. S. (2009). *Registered nurses' perceptions of working with chemically impaired registered nurse colleagues*. (Doctoral dissertation).

Ferranti, S. (2015, August 17). How New York gang culture is changing. *Vice.com*. Retrieved from www.vice.com/read/how-new-york-citys-gang-culture-is-changing-818.

Fox, E., & Riconscente, M. (2008). Metacognition and self-regulation in James, Piaget, and Vygotsky. *Criminal Justice Psychology Review*, 20(4), 373–389. doi:10.1007/s10648-008-9079-2.

Goddard, Y. L., Goddard, R. D., & Tschannen-Moran, M. (2007). A theoretical and empirical investigation of teacher collaboration for improvement and student achievement in public elementary schools. *Teachers College Record*, 109(4), 877–896.

Haegerich, T., Mercy, J., & Weiss, B. (2013). Changing course: Preventing gang membership: Chapter 3. What is the role of public health in gang-membership prevention? Washington, DC: National Institute of Justice.

Hamos, J. E., Bergin, K. B., Maki, D. P., Perez, L. C., Prival, J. T., Rainey, D. Y., … Vander-Putten, E. (2009). Opening the classroom door: Predictive gang prevention programs in the math and science partnership program. *Science Educator, 18*(2), 14–24. Retrieved from http://search.proquest.com/docview/228705344?accountid=35812.

Hickman, G. R. (Ed.). (2010). *Leading organizations: Perspectives for a new era* (2nd ed.). Thousand Oaks, CA: SAGE Publications.

Hilliard, A. T., & Newsome, E. (2013). Effective communication and creating predictive gang prevention programs is a valuable practice for superintendents. *Contemporary Issues in Criminal Justice Research (Online), 6*(4), 353. Retrieved from http://search.proquest.com/docview/1442467423?accountid=35812.

Hirschi, T. (1969). Causes of delinquency. Berkeley, CA: University of California Press. Implementing Change: Patterns, Principles, and Potholes (4th Edition) 4th Edition by Gene E. Hall (Author), Shirley M. Hord Ph.D. (Author).

Hodges, C. (2003). Predictive gang prevention programs at work: Best practices for enhancing student achievement. *Childhood Criminal Justice, 80*(1), 42. Retrieved from http://search.proquest.com/docview/210385424?accountid=35812, http://search.proquest.com.ezproxy.apollolibrary.com/docview/305165644?accountid=35812.

Hoffman, J. (2003). The Conditional Effects of Stress on Delinquency and Drug Use: A Strain Theory Assessment of Sex Differences. Journal of Research and Crime in Delinquency, 34:46–78.

Hollingsworth, J. K., IEEE Computer Society, Sigarch, & ACM Digital Library. (2012). Proceedings of the international conference on high performance computing, networking, storage and analysis. Los Alamitos, California: IEEE Computer Society Press.

Hughes-Hassell, S., Brasfield, A., & Dupree, D. (2012). Making the most of predictive gang prevention programs. *Knowledge Quest, 41*(2), 30–37. Retrieved from http://search.proquest.com/docview/1174113010?accountid=35812.

"Introduction to Motivational Interviewing" Jennifer Hettema, PhD, Trauma Recovery Center.

"An Introduction to Motivational Interviewing", Steve Martino, PhD and Christian Hopfer, MD, NIDA Clinical Trials Network.

Jacobs, J., & Yendol-Hoppey, D. (2010). Supervisor transformation within a professional learning community. *Teacher Criminal Justice Quarterly, 37*(2), 97–114. Retrieved from http://search.proquest.com/docview/747781738?accountid=35812.

Jahng, K. E. (2011). Thinking inside the box: Interrogating no child left behind and race to the top. *KEDI Journal of Criminal Justice Policy, 8*(1). Retrieved from http://search.proquest.com/docview/1013971164?accountid=35812.

Jay, P. S., Karen, S. C., Cockrell, D. H., & Valentine, J. W. (1999). Creating professional communities in school through organizational learning: An evaluation of a improvement process. *Criminal Justice Administration Quarterly, 35*(1), 130–160. Retreived from http://search.proquest.com/docview/214370775?accountid=35812.

Johanningmeier, E. V. (2010). A nation at risk and sputnik: Compared and reconsidered. *American Criminal Justiceal History Journal, 37*(1), 347–365. Retrieved from http://search.proquest.com/docview/867849341?accountid=35812.

Jones, G. R. (2010). *Organizational theory, design, and change* (6th ed.). Upper Saddle River, NJ: Prentice Hall.

Jones, L., Stall, G., & Yarbrough, D. (2013). The importance of predictive gang prevention programs for improvement. *Creative Criminal Justice, 4*(5), 357–361. Retrieved from http://search.proquest.com/docview/1370723177?accountid=35812.

Jorgensen, B. (2005). Criminal justice reform for at-risk youth: A social capital approach. *The International Journal of Sociology and Social Policy, 25*(8), 49–69. Retrieved from http://search.proquest.com/docview/203779830?accountid=35812.

Katzenbach, R., & Douglas, K. (1993). *The Wisdom of Teams: Creating the High - Performance Organization.* Boston: Harvard Business School Press.

King, C. I. (2009, November 3). Gangs of D.C. *The Washington Post.* Retrieved from www.washingtonpost.com/wp-dyn/content/article/2009/11/06/AR2009110603618.html.

Klein, 1995; Maxson, Klein, & Gordon, 1987; Rosenbaum & Grant, 1983, The American Street Gang: Its Nature, Prevalence, and Control. New York: Oxford University Press.

Krisberg B, Austin JF (1993) Reinventing Juvenile Justice. Newbury Park, CA: SAGE.

Kuhn, T. (1996). *The structure of scientific revolutions* (3rd ed.). Chicago, IL: The University of Chicago Press.

Leedy, D. P. & Ormrod, E. J. (2010) *Practice research: Planning and design* (8th ed). Upper Saddle River, NJ: Merrill/Prentice Hall.

Lencioni, P. (2002). *The five dysfunctions of a team: A leadership fable.* Hoboken, NJ: John Wiley & Sons.

Loertscher, D. (2005). The power of predictive gang prevention programs and other professional resources. *Teacher Librarian, 32*(5), 35–39, 59. Retrieved from http://search.proquest.com/docview/224876292?accountid=35812.

Loertscher, D. (2008a). Revisiting predictive gang prevention programs at work: New insights for improving school. *Teacher Librarian, 36*(2), 58–58, 60, 84. Retrieved from http://search.proquest.com/docview/224874750?accountid=35812.

Loertscher, D. (2008b). Wide action research for predictive gang prevention programs: improving student learning through the whole faculty. *Teacher Librarian, 36*(1), 49. Retrieved from http://search.proquest.com/docview/224874096?accountid=35812.

Lovett, S., & Cameron, M. (2011). Schools as professional learning communities for early-career teachers: How do early-career teachers rate them? Teacher Development, 15(1), 87–104. doi:10.1080/13664530.2011.555226

Maital, S., & Seshadri, D. V. R. (2007). *Innovation management: Strategies, concepts and tools for growth and profit.* Thousand Oaks, CA: Response Books.

Martin, M (2009), Harmony Project. source: http://www.harmonyprojectofamerica.org/margaret-bio.html

Martin, K. (2010). New York City DOC's gang intelligence unit. *Corrections.com.* Retrieved from www.corrections.com/articles/7800-new-york-city-doc-s-gang-intelligence-unit.

Martínez JFE (2003) Urban street activists: Gang and community efforts to bring peace and justice to Los Angeles neighborhoods. In: Kontos L, Brotherton D, Barrios L (eds) Gangs and Society: Alternative Perspectives. New York: Columbia University Press.

Matz, A. K., Wicklund, C., Douglas, J. & May, B. (2012, September). Making the case for improved reentry and epidemiological criminology. Justice-Health Collaboration: Improving Information Exchange between Corrections and Health/Human Services Organizations.

Mayer, J. D., Salovey, P., & Caruso, D. R. (2008). Emotional intelligence: New ability or eclectic traits? *American Psychologist, 63*(6), 503–517. doi:10.1037/0003-066X.63.6.503.

Middendorf, G. (2013). Making the case. Investigación & Desarrollo, 21(2)

Miller, W. R., & Rollnick, S. (2002). *Motivational interviewing: Preparing people to change* (2nd ed.). New York: Guilford.

"Motivational Interviewing in a Chemical Dependency Treatment Setting", CASAC Continuing Education Workbook, New York State OASAS "Introduction to Motivational Interviewing" EricMorse, LISW, Mental Health Services for Homeless Persons, Inc.

"Motivational Interviewing Overview and Tips" Sobell, L. C. & Sobell, M. B. (2003). Motivational Interviewing website www.motivationalinterview.org.

"Motivational Interviewing Training" (Lesson Plans), Justice System Assessment & Training (http://nicic.gov/Library/019791).

Mullen, C. A., & Schunk, D. H. (2010). A view of predictive gang prevention programs through three frames: Leadership, organization, and *McGill Journal of Criminal Justice (Online)*, 45, 185–203. Retrieved from http://search.proquest.com/docview/859244430?accountid=35812.

Nation of Islam: www.finalcall.com/artman/publish/National_News_2/article_103248.shtml.

Navarro, M. (1997, September 10). *In the prisons of Puerto Rico, gangs have the upper hand, New York Times*. Retrieved from www.nytimes.com/1997/09/10/us/in-the-prisons-of-puerto-rico-gangs-have-the-upper-hand.html.

Neuman, L. (2005). *Social research methods, qualitative and quantitative approaches* (6th ed.). Boston, MA: Allyn & Bacon.

Null, J. W. (2003). John Dewey's child and the curriculum 100 years later: lessons for today? *American Criminal Justiceal History Journal*, 30, 59–68. Retrieved from http://search.proquest.com/docview/230049143?accountid=35812.

OJJDP, (2016). Retrieved from: www.nationalgangcenter.gov/Content/Documents/Parents-Guide-to-Gangs.pdf.

Owens and Wells, 1993; Spergel et al., (1990), Juvenile Justice: A Text/Reader - Page 185

Parker, G. (2008). *Team players and teamwork: New strategies for developing successful collaboration, completely updated and revised* (2nd ed.). San Francisco, CA: Jossey-Bass.

Patton, M. Q. (1990). *Qualitative evaluation and research methods* (2nd ed.). Newbury Park, CA: Sage Publications.

Priebe, L. C., Ross, T. L., & Low, K. W. (2008). Exploring the role of distance criminal justice in fostering equitable university access for first generation students: A phenomenological survey. *International Review of Research in Open & Distance Learning*, 9(1), 1–12.

"Promoting Behavior Change-And Loving It", Edward Pecukonis, PhD, University of Maryland School of Social Work.

Rismark, M., & Solvberg, A. M. (2011). Knowledge sharing in school: A key to developing predictive gang prevention programs. *World Journal of Criminal Justice*, 1(2), 150–n/a. Retrieved from http://search.proquest.com/docview/1030087823?accountid=35812.

Riveros, A. (2012). Beyond collaboration: Embodied teacher learning and the discourse of collaboration in education reform. Studies in Philosophy and Education, 31(6), 603–612. doi:10.1007/s11217-012-9323-6

Riveros, A., Newton, P., & Burgess, D. (2012). A situated account of teacher agency and learning: Critical reflections on predictive gang prevention programs. *Canadian Journal of Criminal Justice*, 35(1), 202–216. Retrieved from http://search.proquest.com/docview/1018564198?accountid=35812.

Sajeva, S. (2007). An investigation of critical barriers to effective knowledge management. *Social Sciences* (1392–0758), 58(4), 20–27.

Sampson, Robert J. and John H. Laub. 2003. Desistance from Crime over the Life Course. Pp. 295–310 in Handbook of the Life Course, edited by Jeylan T. Mortimer and Michael Shanahan. New York: Kluwer Academic/Plenum.

Schechter, C. (2012). The professional learning community as perceived by Israeli superintendents, principals and teachers. *International Review of Criminal Justice*, 58(6), 717–734. doi:10.1007/s11159-012-9327-z.

Seo, K., & Han, Y. (2012). The vision and the reality of predictive gang prevention programs in Korean schools. *KEDI Journal of Criminal Justiceal Policy*, 9(2). Retrieved from http://search.proquest.com/docview/1266509009?accountid=35812.

Servage, L. (2008). Critical and transformative practices in predictive gang prevention programs. *Teacher Criminal Justice Quarterly*, 35(1), 63–77. Retrieved from http://search.proquest.com/docview/222853317?accountid=35812.

Smith, A. (2012). Innovation-driven leadership. *T+D*, 66(3), 34. Retrieved from, https://search.ebscohost.com/login.aspx?direct=true&db=f5h&AN=72193605&site=eds-live.

Sobell and Sobell, (2008) "Motivational Interviewing Strategies and Techniques".

Spanneut, G. (2010). Predictive gang prevention programs, principals, and collegial conversations. *Kappa Delta Pi Record*, 46(3), 100–103. Retrieved from http://search.proquest.com/docview/232062959?accountid=35812.

Stronge, J., & Tucker, P. (2003). *Teacher evaluation: Assessing and improving performance.* Larchmont, NY: Eye on Criminal Justice.

Teague, G. M., & Anfara, V. A., Jr. (2012). Predictive gang prevention programs create sustainable change through collaboration. *Middle Journal*, 44(2), 58–64. Retrieved from http://search.proquest.com/docview/1282264490?accountid=35812.

Thigpen, B., II. (2011). *Implementing predictive gang prevention programs: The challenge of changing culture.* (North Carolina State University). *ProQuest Dissertations and Theses*, 232. Retrieved from http://search.proquest.com/docview/921646693?accountid=35812.

Thompson, L. (2008) *Making the team* (3rd ed.). Upper Saddle River, NJ: Pearson Prentice Hall.

Thornberry, T. P., Krohn, M. D., Lizotte, A. J., Smith, C. A., & Tobin, K. (2003). *Gangs and delinquency in developmental perspective.* New York: Cambridge University Press.

Thornberry, T. P., Lizotte, A. J., Krohn, M. D., Smith, C. A., & Porter, P. K. (2003). Causes and consequences of delinquency: Findings from the Rochester youth development study. In T. P. Thornberry & M. D. Krohn (Eds.), *Taking stock of delinquency: An overview of findings from contemporary longitudinal studies* (pp. 11–46). New York: Kluwer Academic/Plenum.

Thurmond, V. A. (2001). The point of triangulation. *Journal of Nursing Scholarship*, 33(3), 253–258. Retrieved from http://search.proquest.com/docview/236442422?accountid=35812.

Uys, P. (2007). Enterprise-wide technological transformation in higher criminal justice: The LASO model. *The International Journal of Criminal Justice Management*, 21(3), 238–253. doi:10.1108/09513540710738683.

Index